FUTURISTIC VERSION
OF
GEETA

FUTURISTIC VERSION
— OF —
GEETA

The Ultimate Theory of Fate

P A R K A S H   S A T T I

PARTRIDGE

A Penguin Random House Company

Print information available on the last page.

To order additional copies of this book, contact
Partridge India
000 800 10062 62
orders.india@partridgepublishing.com

www.partridgepublishing.com/india

Contents

About Book

This book is about theory of fate, the very first time this book is revealing the theory of fate; this book will explain how man has bonded with fate, every man and woman bonded with fate, the whole existence has bonded with fate.

This book reveals (sannyasin) renunciation, the most modern manner of living, how renunciation can completely change this entire world? And why this world required (Sannyasin) renunciation? What is the possibility with (Sannyasin) renunciation? What is the real meaning of (sannyasin) renunciation?

If the reader will understand that what the author is trying to explain - the theory of fate and (Sannyasin) renunciation, so there is no further requirement left to read this book. The whole essence of this book is in the starting chapters, theory of fate and the (Sannyasin) renunciation most modern manner of living.

Do not miss a single word of these chapters and read them very carefully; this book has potential to change your whole world, if you can understand it. You have to surrender yourself during the reading, if you will not allow this book to teach you so there is no way that this book can change you.

This book just demands your complete attention, consideration, you have to surrender yourself during the reading, if you will not allow this book to teach you so there is no way that this book can change your opinion. Every new idea needs permission to accept it if the opinion would welcome with the open mind, so there is the possibility with the new idea, although acceptance and rejection depend on every individual, but the thoughts have gone deeply.

This book reveals sculpture worship, what is the science behind of this sculpture worship culture.

This book will reveal the great sutras of Geeta and give them new definition.

This book reveals devotion, worship, love, fear, and fashion and their real meanings.

This book will reveal about (Kundalini) 7 Chakra awakening, not only this, the simple and straight recipe of kundalini awakening has revealed.

This book is the revealing definition of the God, what is the God? All the misconception about the God,

This book reveals the real possibility of man's mind, what state possibly man can achieve by meditation.

Theory of fate

Chapter-3, Shlok-5

na hi kascit ksanam api jatu tisthaty akarmakrt
karyate hy avasah karma sarvah prakrti-jair gunaih

One cannot remain without engaging in activities at any
time, even for a moment;
Certainly all living entities are helplessly compelled to
action by the qualities endowed by material nature

Chapter – 3, Shlok – 27

prakrteh kriyamanani gunaih karmani sarvasah
ahankara-vimudhatma kartaham iti manyate

All activities are being enacted by the senses of the
material nature without exception;
But the unrealized, deluded by false identification of being
the body, thus thinks: "I'm the doer"

This shlok has whole Geeta's essence, juice; this shlok
completes Geeta and its further chapters.

But in the further chapters Lord Krishna has explained
in the different-different ways and words,

This chapter will explain all; how one Sanskrit Shlok
developed in great theory, this is very first time that a book
has revealed the theory of fate. Just be patient and read it
very carefully.

We all are bonded with material nature; it all started
from starting according to scientific theory.

"Theory of fate"

Theory of present science

The subatomic particles included protons, neutrons, and electrons. Though simple atomic nuclei formed within the first three minutes after the Big Bang thousands of years passed before the first electrically neutral atoms formed. The majority of atoms produced by the Big Bang were hydrogen, along with helium and traces of lithium.

Giant clouds of these primordial elements later coalesced to form stars and galaxies through gravity, and the heavier elements were synthesized either within stars or during supernovae.

The big bang theory offers a comprehensive explanation for a broad range of observed phenomena.

This is how all started.

Theory of Hindu Veda's (Santana Dharma)

According to Hindu Vedas (Sanatan dharma) says, this universe created from the navel (which is a single point) of Vishnu, described as a lotus blooming out of the navel, much like our big bang universe.

This is how all started.

Both present science and Veda's language are totally different, but in the end, both come into the same conclusion.

"I'm telling you the theory of fate, read it very carefully"

Scientists talk about the Big Bang, they talk about subatomic particles included protons, neutrons, and electrons and high energy. Although no scientist can answer that where all these particles came from, from where this much force came, maybe one day in the future some group of scientist would find out from where all this started.

Vedas says, this universe came from the navel of Vishnu, according to Vedas Lord Vishnu would have decided that how much power, how much energy this universe required to come into existence, how this universe and it's all stars, it's all plants, whatever in this universe is, its size, shape and behavior will be, "suppose there is a robot that could calculate accurately. A robotic arm, which could throw the ball with exact a hundred KM per hour speed. The machine should be capable of selecting the exact angle and exact measure for the direction of the ball, it could measure the air pressure, it could calculate where the ball will fall, when the ball will reach to its destination, the machine could predict all details, the machine could predict where the ball will reach, it is possible with today's technology.

But something that machine cannot predict that what will happen with the ball, where the ball possibly will fall, on water or a dry place or a person. Suppose a comet falls in the same place and destroy the ball, so this machine cannot predict, but to understand the fate of the ball, we have to go back to the first action of The Big bang, from where all this started.

After the Big bang if this could calculate where all the material is going, and this keeps calculating until this robotic arm throws the ball so by calculating bit by bit this could be predictable that where this comet will fall,

And this Big bang reaction also decides that someone who build this robotic arm, he will build or not, he will release the ball or not, if release so what will happen to this ball, it is all related to the first action of Big bang.

This is how fate works, it is the chain reaction, maybe in future machine can predict every moment before it happens,

You must be thinking how man is bonding with fate? Whether man can predict or not, but one thing is true that this whole existence bonded with fate, which I will prove in my theory of fate.

After, two more examples the complete theory of fate has given."

"**S**uppose you have few small rocks, if you throw them so one could go far, one will not go, so are rocks having any control in this? No. Rocks will reach till where, the force was used to throw them. Although these rocks will reach on the place till where this force takes them, if one is running fast, so does not mean that the rock did anything special in this, it is the throwing force applying to throw them, in the same way the power the force was used in the creation of this universe, according to that this universe has taken its shape and size, and all the planets, all the stars, all the galaxies took their shape,"

"**A**nother example, in an empty room if we take one balloon and measure its size, its shape, and its material, and there should be a machine, which can calculate everything, like, if this balloon will blast with pressure air, so where its material will spread and with what pace. If this machine can calculate and predict this that how it would all happen,

When this Big Bang happened so when all the material was spreading so it was spreading, according to the force has given to its particles, if the force were different so this whole universe would be different, but in pursuance of its force this universe has created like this. As we see it, all the galaxies created, all the stars, and all the plants created, in pursuance of that our own solar system created, our planet, the moon and all other planets created,"

Big Bang power could be different more or less. This world could be different; all the universe could be different. There would not have any earth here, and there would not be you. But it had to happen in the way, so it happened, and this event created this whole universe and this earth, it created all the material, created our world, created man and woman, every creature everything, as we know on this planet and outside of it.

Every action has its reaction, so big bang's action has its reaction; it is our universe, it is all the human kind, it is me, everything as we know yet, one action created this earth and the earth gave chance to thrive in life.

Doesn't matter life created here itself or it came from outer space, because planet earth was favorable for life, so life thrived here.

And then, according to this planet's weather life developed here, land, trees, animals, rivers, oceans, birds, human, every creature everything, whatever is existed in here on this planet earth, it is all because of that starting, because of the Big Bang and the way it happened, all these events are related to each other, because that Big Bang happened, that is why this is happening, it is the reaction of that starting action.

With time human race developed, it happened in according to the weather and atmosphere of the earth.

The theory of fate starts from here.

When A and B give birth to −C, how Child C will be? It is all depend on personality of A, the kind of person A would be, and similarly the seed would be, educate or illiterate, open mind or orthodox, the kind of relation he has with society, the kind of relation he has with his wife, his whole personality's impact falls on his sperm and when he will do meeting with a woman and leave his seed inside her, it would be the half step of his creation,

(Mother-B) "Seed of A will develop in womb of B" what kind of Child-C will take birth it depends, what kind of person Mother-B would be, what kind of relation she has with father-A of Child-C, what she has in her interior according to that, Seed-C will develop and take birth as a child in this world and the atmosphere provide by his parents A and B.

Now go backward

The father-A of Child-C, A-his nature and his development depended on his parents. What kind of person A's father was and his mother was according to that child-A born, and the atmosphere provided by his parents, Father's seed and mother's womb and the atmosphere gave by them to Child-A, all this gave a shape to Child-A, he developed accordingly all these,

And according to A's development, A chose his wife and left his impact on his wife, and he created and attracted world toward his side, which made a kind of atmosphere in which his child taken birth.

Back to A's father and mother, how was A's father was, it was all depend on A's grandparents, the gene (DNA) transfer generation to generation and according to that atmosphere made and, whatever upcoming generation doing, they are doing accordingly their Gene (DNA) creation.

So it is totally clear that human does not have any control on his doing or his decisions, anything they do or think all is their fate.

This theory of fate applies on whole existence, whatever in this whole existence has bonded with fate.

So when a couple gave birth to a child, child born with the abilities, those abilities, his father and his mother carrying in them, the child carried forward his parents' gene. The child does not have any control on his birth and development. The seed of a man of his sperm and womb of his mother, the seed will develop according to the womb of his mother, according to the atmosphere his parents provide to the child he will develop and that atmosphere will give child a right shape for his development.

"Example- **If** the raw material would feel in the molding machine, what this material will come out as? It will come out according to the shape of molding machine, if the molding machine is square material will come out in a square shape, if it is a rectangle or triangle materials will come out as a rectangle or as a triangle shape.

In the same way, as the atmosphere and gene parents pass on to the child, according to that child will develop. These codes of DNA will develop whole personality of child. All the decisions and actions will take accordingly his DNA Coding, and according to this his growth will be.

All the thoughts will come down accordingly his DNA coding. The point of view toward this world and point of view toward things, toward life. It entirely depends on his DNA Coding. Whatever its inside same will come down outside, your interiority is your exteriority. So child's whole nature, his all actions, his all decisions will be according to DNA Coding, according to his interiority. Your exteriority is a reflection of your interiority. When this child will grow up. When he chooses his job, his friends, his life partner, all that he will choose, all selection will happen according to its interiority. The decision cannot be anything else, cannot be different. Whatever he received from his parents, the gene, the atmosphere according to that, according to fate, this child's fate will give shape to his life. Whatever his parents pass on to him, whatever atmosphere they have given to him, this will be the blueprint for his life. If you have Red in your interiority, so your exterior matter will be Red. Your decision will be Red; it can't be Green or yellow or black. Every thought of yours, every opinion of yours, the whole nature of yours, the whole being of yours will follow the footprint of your interiority. Whatever code has decoded in you that makes you, only you. Whatever you are doing, you did or you will do, it all have decided millions of million years ago, your whole being has decided by the first action of this existence. You cannot be anybody else, the cause of your whole being is your fate, the fate made by your DNA Codes and your DNA Codes are an event of the chain reaction of the very first event of this universe, of this existence that is the Big Bang.

Man is not doer, man is just an event, which just happened in this existence, so if you think your success or your failure is yours, then this is not true,

If one is short temper and other is calm, so does not mean it is because of them, they do not have any reduction and skillfully in this, so they are not reason of their lacking or merit. Whatever is happening in their life, had to happen, that is why it is happening. In this way good is not good and bad is not bad, both are equal, it is just they are doing what they can do; they are following instruction of their codes.

I have asked many time, many questions, people argue with me about the theory of fate,

Those questions I have asked are here,

People put up questions, when I say whatever happens in your life, it is because of fate, one thing is very difficult that is truth, digesting truth is the most difficult thing in this world. This is not easy for everyone, man's arrogance stops him doing this, when they argue with me and I explain them every time everything about fate, so in spite of that they put up more questions, like,

(1) If anybody born as dumb child, and the child will do meditation and Yoga, so why cannot he improves? They say! Doing yoga and meditation is in a man's hands; this is

not related to fate, what fate will do with this? If they want to do this, they can do.

(Answer) Yes, if anybody will do meditation and Yoga, so he or she can improve, I agree.

But the thing is, why does anybody choose meditation or yoga? Why did only some people choose something? Why all other chooses different things?

If Parkash Satti chooses Yoga and Meditation, so why does he only choose them. From where this thought came into his mind that he should do Mediation and Yoga, if anybody told him about this, so why did he only listen. Not everyone listens everything, not everyone likes doing Yoga and Meditation. Think again, whatever is happening in man's life is action's reaction, it is all related to each other, it is a chain reaction. Why Parkash was available to listen? Why someone told him about Yoga and Meditation, because it is fate, think deeply.

(2) One more question this is a very childish question, I have asked many times, if there is food on the plate, so you have to eat by yourself, it will not go into your mouth by itself. In this case, what fate will do with this?

(Answer) Because you are hungry this is why you have food in your plate, because you wanted to eat, that is why this thought came into your mind, if your mind will think that you should not eat this food, because somebody somewhere will be hungry and you give your food to someone who in need, this would your decision. You can think anything, but all that thought come into your mind, those thoughts do not produce by your desire, it is a pattern of your mind, which generates your all thoughts. This pattern of your mind, made by your past experience and present atmosphere. So according to your DNA code your mind attach with the world.

Control of Your mind is not in your hands, how your DNA code designs your mind. It is as simple as a magnet attracts the iron, in the same way, according to your gene you attract to the things and design your mind. That is your fate.

Because this is your nature, you are emotional; you care about people, because you grew up like this, you blessed by this nature by your parents and family, their gene passed on you.

Although not everyone takes same decision, others can be cruel, that is all depend on their family and atmosphere given by their parents.

I don't want to disappoint you, but I want to aware you, once you will be aware of the theory of fate, you will become a different man, your whole life will change, your point of view to society will change. The humanity will grow strongly in man.

Whenever I talk to people, everyone has different-different views, opinion about life, but no one knows the truth, some say, there is not fate, no luck, nothing is like this. The man has to efforts to do things by himself, if you think the man is doer, so you have to change your point of view. The chapatti is ready but nobody will put it in your mouth you have to eat by yourself, if you are sick, you have to go to the doctor and take medicine, without doctor and medicine one could not recover from sickness.

Again, same thing, you will eat food if you are hungry, if you are not you will not. The human being must eat to live, because the structure of the man makes like this.

About the taking medicine, I don't say, you will recover by yourself from sickness without taking medicine. You have to go to the doctor and you have to take the medicine without the medicine you will not recover, but the thing is, if you can pay the fee of doctor then you will be able to go to the doctor. The selection of the doctor depends on his fee, the poor and rich patient will choose accordingly doctor's charges. The man can get success become rich, but man does not have control of his birth. He will be born rich or poor; he will be born intelligent or dumb. A child does not have a choice of his birth, that all depends on his parents, and in his future he will become successful or failure, it all depends what is in the child. The design of his mind will choose, what kind of person he will become.

The man does not have any control over his thoughts, all these thoughts come by itself, all the thought, design according to man's nature and his nature design according to his DNA and atmosphere given by his family and parents.

Some people imprecate God, why God made them poor and helpless, why they are not intelligent, why they are not beautiful, why they are not tall, why life is so cruel to them, life is journey it always continues, we are playing a character in which we don't have any control.

This world can become a much better place, intelligence has a great potential, and it can open new ways to this society, and these new ways can bring the peace, happiness and beauty in this world.

And then this society does not deal with hate, this society does not require any prison, this society does not need to punish people beside of punishment this society has to provide right education, the right education will completely remove crime from this society.

If the right and complete knowledge would give to man, so this society will be the different place, but first man has to accept the truth, this truth will bring wisdom and wisdom will bring happiness.

Once man accepts and understands this theory of fate, so the action of man will be totally different,

The teaching of (Sannyasin) renunciation, the most modern manner of living, this most modern manner of living can bring great changes in this whole society, the world. In the next chapter you will be reading in details.

There is one incident I remember.

One day I received an invitation from Christian missionary to visiting the Church.

he who gave me the invitation, he tried to explain me that why everyone should be the Christian, whosoever is Christian will go to heaven, and can live special life and will be blessed by God and Jesus son of God.

I accepted his invitation; I went to the church, they said, if I will come to the church regularly my life will change, God will bless me, I wanted to see that what kind of changes can come in me and my life.

I reached the church in the service, they were saying that Christianity is a great and true religion and it is only truth. Son of God came into this world for us and sacrificed his only son Jesus for mankind, after crucify Jesus came back for mankind, whosoever will become Christian will go to Heaven and will be blessed by the son of God, Jesus and God, they said, Christianity is not a religion, there was nothing new for me, every religion says that their religion is greater than all other religions and their religion is only true religion and all other religion, nothing were new for me.

So in the service they asked me, do I accept Jesus and do I agree to believe in Jesus and Christianity?

I was quiet, what could I have supposed to spoken that time, I stayed put, there were many people in the church that time, I did not want to embarrass to the Pastor of the church, because I had known, if I will speak a single word so their shop could close, so I thought I should better shut my mouth,

Pastor said I have to repeat behind him what he speaks and then he said he is praying for me, he said he will speak in other language and then he gave me something, they call bread, he asked me to put the bread in my mouth and then he said, I have become a Christian, I was totally shocked that what has exactly happened and what is the meaning of become a Christian, they were trying to impose their religion on me, I just went there to see, how they do pray and as he told me with big confidence like he is giving me guaranty that my life will change, because the time they invited me, they spoken big words, I was still thinking, about changing life, but I did not know what have happened, I didn't say a word, he said, he will pray for me, if I have any problem, he will pray to God and whatever Devil has done wrong in my life, so God will change, and make my life better, they said, I can ask anything whatever in my mind,

But I didn't say anything, they were getting irritate with me that I'm not asking anything, and saying no to everything and I was controlling to myself not to open my mouth,

Because, if I will open my mouth. So they won't be able to give the answer to my single question. If I will open my mouth so they will repent that why they invited me into the church, so I stayed them happy, they were happy that they have gathered few more puppets for church, and now only they have to follow them up that they will not distract and keep coming to the church and keep collecting their knowledge which has become junk now, left no meaning. So they keep calling me to the church and asked me to be regular in the church, but I was just not going to the church, the pastor always told me that I'm missing something very precious,

One day the pastor of the church, he was telling me that I will go to Heaven because I have become Christian and those are not Christian will not go to Heaven, they said I should not miss the Sunday church, I should always come to the church and get Jesus' blessings, he said this is the reason that we are informing more and more people, as much as people we can, to accept Christianity, to become Christian that they also can get Jesus' blessings and go to Heaven.

I said what about those who you could not inform yet about Christianity, what about them?

If they will not become Christian, so will they not go to Heaven? What about them? What are their mistakes in this? He said that's why me and our Christian people spreading Bible and calling people to the church and informing them about Christianity,

I asked, what do you think, will you reach to everyone? He replied we are trying to reach the maximum number of people, maximum but not everyone, so those you will not reach will not go to Heaven, he didn't say no, he said, who is Christian will go to Heaven, I asked so who will take responsibility on this?

Many people will die without knowing this, that they can go to Hell because they are not Christian, if they could become Christian, so they could have gone to Heaven, so who is responsible for this, I said, according to your theory, your God is doing partiality with them, to not giving place them in the Heaven without Christianity, and also it is your fault, because you are failure so you should go to Hell for this, because you all have got failed to spread Christianity to everyone,

You all should go to Hell, for not to inform them, that because they are not Christian, so they will go to Hell and rotten there. Because it's you who told me about this, so according to you, you are aware of everything and you should rotten in Hell, he got so shocked, after that day, he never called me in the service of the church; he has understood that it is not his cup of tea convincing me.

Shri Krishna said in Geeta.

All activities are being enacted by the senses of the material nature without exception; but the unrealized, deluded by false identification of being the body, thus thinks: "I'm the doer"

So man's uselessly arrogance, his ego that he is the doer, has not any meaning, it is totally reasonless, and the reasoned of all arrogance is his ignorance, lack of wisdom, a wise man never takes credit of his success or his failure. Living life in pain has no reason, if you know that you don't have any control in your life or others life, you cannot even control your thoughts, they are coming according to its nature, according to its pattern, so you can be happiest man or woman in this world, you can live life in balance because there is no other way of living,

As long as you will force yourself, you will drag yourself into the hell, where you will live a life what you have already lived.

When I say Hell I don't mean that man-made fictitious the Hell and the Heaven, I refer to the condition of human life,

As I have given the theory of fate, so it proves there is no heaven and hell, whatever fear is created by man is false. The man does not have any control on his hand, every man, woman the whole existence bonded with fate, it means nobody is evil and good, there is no sin and virtue, there is no good and evil.

Ch-3, 8- You should perform your
prescribed Vedic activities since actions
are better than renouncing actions;
by ceasing activity even your bodily
maintenance will not possible.

Conclusion – No one should run away from his duties, this Shlok simply explaining this.

Ch-4, Sh-13-The four divisions of
the human order were created by me
according to differences in quality,
activities, and aptitude; although
the creator of this, know me as
the non-doer being invariable.

Conclusion – When Lord Krishna said, "By me" he is always meant by nature, Lord Krishna is not separate from

Parkash Satti

nature; man is not separate from nature, every living and non-living things are not separated from nature, everything is part of God, in fact, everything thing is God, it is just man does not know, and one more thing is mentioned in the shlok, he knows everything but still he is non-doer, so how can a man become the doer.

The whole existence is bound by this nature, bonded with fate. If man would understand this sutra, there would be no problems left; there would be no pain and misery left.

> Ch-5, Sh-14-The ultimate consciousness neither creates human misconceptions of bodily identification; nor the bodily identification certain activities; nor the union of the certain actions and the resulting fruits; but it is due to the modes of material nature, engaging in acts.

Conclusion – this Sutra gives the reference that man has bonded with material senses, he also bonded with fate.

> Ch-18, Sh-19-Knowledge, action and the doer are described in the Vedic scriptures as three kinds only according to the different modes of material nature, now hear about these as well in due order.

Conclusion – every quality man has, it is given by material nature, man does not need to be egoistic.

20-Understand that knowledge by which one undivided, imperishable reality is seen within all diverse living entities is in the nature of goodness.

Conclusion – Which generates all wisdom and the truth, that calls pure truth.

21-But that knowledge by which one experience separated diversity within all living entities, variety in quality, and plurality in essence; understand that knowledge as in the nature of passion.

Conclusion – only with pure wisdom man sees truth, man find the equalities in all the human being.

> Ch-16, 5- The divine nature is
> considered the cause of liberation
> and the demoniac nature the cause
> of bondage; do not worry, O Arjuna,
> you are born of the divine nature.

Conclusion – The bad qualities are the bond of man, these qualities are the reason of man's misery and good qualities make man free from all the sin, now it is up to man what does he choose, although the choice is out of man's hands.

> Ch-18, 15, 16, 17-

> Whatever action a being performs by the
> body, speech and mind, whether proper or
> improper; these five factors are its cause.

> But such being the case, then one who
> sees the embodied self as the doer,
> that ignorant being devoid of any
> spiritual intelligence realizes nothing.

One whose mentality never considers
being the does and whose spiritual
intelligence is not attached to certainty
such a person even if warring with the
whole; does not actually slay anyone
nor become entangled by certainty.

Conclusion – Man eats, but he is not one who eats, man speaks, but he is not a speaker, man sees, but he is not an eye, man is doing, but he is not a doer, the reason of all things, reason of whole existence is God, and man is not separated from God, God is both man's interior and exterior.

Ch-2, 47, 48- You certainly have the
right for prescribed activities but never
at any time in their results. You should
never be motivated by the results of the
actions, nor should be any attachment
in not doing your prescribed activities.

O Arjuna, established in the science of
yoga in action, perform your activities
giving up attachment and become
equipoise in both success and failure.
This equanimity is known as the science
of uniting the individual consciousness
with the ultimate consciousness.

Conclusion – Balance, equipoise! Equipoise yours every deed, being equipoise is the aim of this life, the whole existence stands by balance.

Sannyasin

The most modern manner of living

Science is not much far from renunciation (Sannyasin), if science joins hand with sannyasin, renunciation, so science will achieve height, which never imagines in human history, it would open a new chapter for this world, but the ignorance of society is pushing away to (sannyasin) renunciation, this world has misconceptions about (Sannyasin) renunciation; this society has completely changed the meaning of (Sannyasin) renunciation.

Definition of Sannyasin

Renunciation (Sannyasin) is the most modern manner of living, the extremely large requirement of this society is renunciation (sannyasin), without sannyasin this society has come to the edge of collapsing, this society and this world did not survive without sannyasin, and this is the last resort for humankind. All the balance of the society has lost,

Yet this world believes that sannyasin is a thing that someone does in the ending years of his life, and only old people can take sannyasin, or should take sannyasin, renunciation (sannysin) has become the thing of old age people, and few people made (sannyasin) renunciation their business, they are selling sannyasin. And the generation of today feels bored hearing about (sannyasin) renunciation, there is no respect left for (sannyasin) renunciation.

I want to introduce sannyasin (renunciation) to this world; introduce to the youngsters, to the child, to the man and woman, sannyasin is not that what people believe and understand,

One who does not involve in any religion, one who does not involve in cast system, one who is practical, one who does not interfere in others life, one who does not bond with rotten rule rituals, one who does not resist to anything, one who is pure being, one who is totally original, one who does not manipulate himself for anybody or any fashion,

Recluse (Sannyasi) just flow with life no resistance left at all, that is it, there is no other definition of sannyasin,

Wearing (sannyasi) recluse's costume, grow beard, wear necklaces, leave your home, stay away from the world and do not get married and become brahmacharya, all these have nothing to do with (sannyasin) renunciation,

If this education of sannyasin spread and teach to new and upcoming generation so there would be no problems left in this world, this whole world will totally change.

Once there was a man and he was about 30 years old, his name was Bhajma and he was (sannyasi) recluse, he was a Jovian person, he did not care about rotten society and did not follow society's rotten rules and regulations, people always talked about him behind his back, whenever people spoke to him he replied them from (sannyasin) renunciation's point of view and his point of view was very different than others.

But his lifestyle does not match his words, he totally looked a like a regular person, but the people around him cannot digest this, even his relatives cannot digest this, but Bhajman's family was different they neither supported him, nor against him, Bhajman's neighbor and relatives asked his family why does not he get married his age is going, whenever his relatives meet him, they asked him hundreds of questions and few of them give him their rubbish advice,

One day one of his uncles visited his home, Bhajman was going to meet his friend, and his uncle asked him where are you going? He replied going to a friend's place, without wasting a second his uncle start giving him his old and nonsense lecture and asked him many questions what are you doing these days, why are you wasting your time and nothing will happen with this (Sannyasin) renunciation thing, find out some good job and get married, start your family, taking (sannyasin) renunciation is not easy, one has to do body mortification and it would take years, he was boring him with his nonsense lecture, he was just hearing to him quietly without saying a word.

Actually, his uncle's and people around him, their problem was his lifestyle, his happiness and his satisfying nature, he seems to them atheist and he does not care them like other relatives do, they did never digest his calm and relaxed life, after listening all his uncle's nonsense talked, he asked him a question in the language in which he could understand, Uncle as you know very well I wanted to become a (sannyasi) recluse, what is your advice? How to become (sannyasi) recluse? How do (sannyasi) recluse look alike? What is sannyasi, recluse's recognizance?

His uncle got so proud and happy for himself that Bhajma was asking his advice, the guy who always gives everyone speech on (sannyasin) renunciation, today asking him about (sannyasin) renunciation, his uncle started telling him about renunciation. Recluse's recognizance is who wears orange or ordinary clothes, who wears ear coil, who wears Tilak on his forehead, who is vegetarian, who never use liquor, lives in the ashram and follows bramcharya,(who take oath not to do sex for his life time) is sannyasi, recluse, this the identification of (sannysi) recluse.

Next day he called his uncle and told him that he has decided that he will take (sannyasin) renunciation, his uncle was shocked and he inform other relatives too, everybody reached his home where they found that he having the same getup what his uncle told him, he said, he is going to Haridwar and take (sannyasin) renunciation, he was ready to move because he adopted (sannyasin) renunciation, so he is worth of worship so his uncle greeting him and gave some money, so others relatives followed his uncle and gave him money too,

In few days everybody forgot this incident and got busy in their life and after few days he came back to home, and his returning action spread news faster than fire, so his uncle came to him and he was both so angry and very much happy, he was angry because he has given him money and lied to him, and he was happy because he proved right that (sannyasin) renunciation is not that easy and not everybody can become a (sannyasi) recluse.

He came and started on him, he stopped his uncle and asked him why he seems so upset, his uncle asked him, why? Don't you know why I'm upset? he replied, no I don't know, his uncle said because you left (sannyasin) renunciation, and again adopted mundane culture, wore regular clothes, if you were not able to follow sannyasin, so why did you lied to us all? This is why I'm upset with you, Bhajma replied, so you mean when I was going to Haridwar and adopted a recluse's costume, so I was (sannyasi) recluse and now you saying that I have left (sannyasin) renunciation, because I renounce (sannyasin) renunciation's costume, his uncle said yes right."

So you are saying that whosoever will wear a recluse's costume become (sannyasi) recluse, so sannyasin is all about costume and lifestyle, so by this means anybody who wears the ordinary or orange costume will become (sannyasi) recluse, (Sannyasin) renunciation is not about wear or taking off the costume.

I did not leave (sannyasin) renunciation, it is also not about renouncing mundane things-worldly things, it is also not about taking initiation of any guru, sannyasin, renunciation is awakening of you being, (sannyasin) renunciation is happiness of your interiority, sannysin is calm, sannyasin is satisfactory of your interiority, it is like dip in the Ganges and get completely pure, this dip also make your soul totally pure, in renunciation you does not need to renounce mundane things, it does not matter at all, matter what are you wearing, where are you living, what do you do, what is your job, what do you eat or what not to eat, you are married or unmarried, (sannyasin) renunciation means awakening, whoever awake calls (sannyasi) recluse, renunciation is not a thing that you can take from somebody or buy it, it is an event that can happen and anybody who tries for it can happen with him and her, as you cannot buy love or cannot borrow love from anybody, in the same way (sannyasin) renunciation happen, you can't borrow or buy it, you can say, fall in (sannyasin) renunciation,

This sentence fall in love is really beautiful, when everything falls then love happens. When your entire arrogance, hate, orthodoxy, misconception, madness falls, then love happens, then (Sannyasin) renunciation happens.

"So when" everything falls then (sannyasin) renunciation happens in you. Sannyasin does not mean to resist things or renounce them, (sannyasin) renunciation means to flow with wave no resistance when all resistance disappears, so sannyasin happens, and then the flower of your being blooms, not one flower, millions of millions flowers blooms inside you.

And then Bhajma said it was a lesson for all of you, and the money you gave I spent all in the tour of Haridwar, and I went there because I feel like to have some time alone, I thought this would be a good idea. You are getting bothered without any reason, I have explained to you many times, do not interfere others life.

In our society old sannyasin, renunciation has made big confusion, the ancient knowledge has lost only body left, just hollow knowledge left, its deep sense has lost, just superficial knowledge left, people has forgotten the meaning of (sannyasin) renunciation, only orthodox people live in today's time, otherwise Indian culture is so rich and beautiful,

And People like Bhajma's uncle they never peep into their own life but stay busy digging others life, what others doing or what not doing, why they are doing, and they keep ill will for others success, they jealous of others happiness, they do not much bother about their own life, if they make time to think about their own life, they will know, what they are doing and what the motive of this life is, where their life is going, how they are living their life, and what possibility of their life is.

(Sannyasin) Renunciation simply means liberation, happiness, and balance, (sannyasin) renunciation never resists life to open the new possibility, never resist to happiness and freedom, and there is no rule in renunciation (sannyasin),

Its only meaning is flowing with the wave of life, flow with the wave of freedom, flow with the wave of joy, and flow with the wave of balance. No resistance at all completely liberation,

but today's sannyasin, renunciation meaning totally has changed, people who believe that they are (sannyasi) recluse, they are just mannequins of rules and rigidity, and these mannequins cannot be (sannyasi) recluse, and they cannot lead you toward right path of (sannyasin) renunciation, they can only give you rules and rigidness.

Because for them sannyasin, renunciation is just renounce Mandan things and until our society stay in this misunderstand, the society would not be able to achieve freedom and happiness of (Sannyasin) renunciation, just orthodoxy society will stay.

And all misconception will be in our society about (sannyasin) renunciation, misconception like, if anyone is (sannyasi) recluse so he or she has to renounce his/her family, he cannot get married if unmarried, he cannot do a job or business, cannot make friends, cannot celebrate, just meditate and chanting the God's name and spend his whole life with apathetic, cold, sad, boring, but this is not true, this absolutely wrong idea about (sannyasin) renunciation.

Renunciation (Sannyasin) is opposite of all these thoughts. Meaning of (sannyasin) renunciation is the celebration in every bit of your life, renunciation is joy, renunciation is happiness, renunciation is an enthusiast, renunciation is the most modern manner of living, and renunciation (sannyasin) is a great way of truth, way of intelligence, way of wisdom, and renunciation (sannyasin) is a path of awakening.

Renunciation is the science of great living, renunciation is an ancient science, which teaches us the most modern manner of living.

Everybody should be sannyasi, recluse, because it is path of intelligence only intelligent people can understand (sannyasin) renunciation, this is a thing of the intellectual human being.

To understand (sannyasin) renunciation, the world will have to take it very seriously, otherwise this world, this civilization will collapse because of human behavior, and one-day human behavior will lead this world to the destruction, and our civilization already has seen two world wars.

Before this human behavior would ruin everything, man has to learn the most modern manner of living (Sannyasin) renunciation, renunciation (sannyasin) is only hoped for this civilization to escape from this misery and destruction.

"If anybody asks me about Sannyasin renunciation, in very few words I would say.

Renunciation (Sannyasin) is liberation, Sannyasin is resistance free, the sannyasin is complete freedom and completely resistance free.

Liberation from everything; sannyasin is free from all kinds of resistance, in (sannyasin) renunciation no resistance left at all.

Meaning of sannyasin is free from all religion, all rituals, all relations, and all mundane things; in sannyasin no bond and boundaries left total freedom.

Renunciation (Sannyasin) means just flow with the wave of your soul, flow with God, just flow with your interior deep core, just flow with love, just fall in love with (sannyasin) renunciation,

When (sannyasin) renunciation happens so all kinds of resistance disappear, in presence of (sannyasin) renunciation all kinds of resistance disappear and the whole liberation come into presence.

One can do anything whatever he or she wants to do, this is what the sannyasin is all about.

The most modern manner of living.

Soul and Mind

The man is a soul, but he lived his life as mind, the reason behind of this is the teaching, which provided for man by his parents, teachers, family, society. The man has to absorb in the soul, but he is absorbed in the mind.

The soul is total intelligence and the mind is material. The man completely disconnected with soul, many (sannyasi) recluses try to connect man with soul, intelligence, but habit of man to stick to mind material is not let him connect with the soul,

The mind is hardware and the soul is software, without the software hardware is totally irrelevant, waste, because of the soul human mind runs but still both are disconnected to each other. The meeting of mind and soul calls awakening, consciousness.

All the wrong decisions made by mind, no (sannyasi) recluse made the cause of distraction, all the distractions made by the mind, the whole world is suffering because of the imbalance, the balance will come with combination of mind and soul, intelligence and material.

There was a Greedy man, he always dreamed about treasure, he wants to become rich, he was ordinary trader, this is about a thousand years old story, one day during his trading journey he met a fakir, the fakir reads his palm lines and predicted about him that he will become very rich and he will find a great treasure, the greedy man asked, when I will find this treasure, I dreamed about this treasure since very long time.

The fakir told him to go toward the east direction about a hundred miles further near the pair of pond side of the

Piple tree, as a fakir told, he went in the same direction and found the treasure, and came back with it.

With the treasure he bought the massive land and build his palace, there was every facility in his palace, it was not an ordinary palace it was like town, he had thousands of servants, but when he bought this land and constructed, during the construction of his palace he cut a big part of the forest, he also changed the direction of the river. He was living with his family and thousands of servants happily,

Everything was great, but after few months, slowly-slowly things started changing, the whole town dearth, many people died and thousands of animals died, his all servants moved from there and all the animal moved from there, because he cut a big part of the forest and he changed the direction of the river, this happened, when the whole place got empty that the greedy man left alone, although he has everything his all treasure, but he died after all this, because Gold diamond cannot save the man.

Illiteracy always brings problems, but the right education can bring happiness. When I say education so I always mean education of sannyasin.

> Ch-3, Sh-4-A person can never achieve
> freedom from reactions to activities
> without first performing prescribed
> Vedic duties; neither can perfection be
> attained by renouncing them as well.

Conclusion – Man's lies has become his enemy, the event of (sannyasin) renunciation happens in your interior, it couldn't happen to your exterior, your interior event's action's reaction comes on your exteriority in your whole personality, this different point of view changes whole being of man.

> Ch-3, Sh-6-Anyone who having
> controlled the five working sense
> organs remains thinking within the
> mind about sense objects, that foolish
> being is known as a hypocrite.

Conclusion - In the presence of lies, truth disappears, in the presence of renunciation (sannyasin) lies cannot stay. (Sannyasin) renunciation is truth, (Sannyasin) renunciation purifies human.

> Ch-4, sh-36- Even if you are the
> most sinful of all sinners; yet you will
> cross over all sins and miseries by the
> boat of transcendental knowledge.

Conclusion – Dip of (sannyasin) renunciation makes a man totally purifies. It does not matter what kind of life he or she has lived.

> 37- O Arjuna, just as a blazing fire
> turns wood to ashes; similarly, the
> fire of knowledge turns all reactions
> from certain activities to ashes.

Conclusion – only path of wisdom can give man bright future, otherwise there is no other hope for man.

Ch-5, sh-3- It should be known, O
mighty armed one, that one who neither
disdains nor desires the fruits of actions
is always a renunciation; certainly that
person being free from all dualities
is easily liberated from bondage.

Conclusion – (Sannysi) Recluse stays equipoise in all conditions. Because only balanced life can make happy and liberate.

4- The unintelligent say that renunciation
of action and prescribed actions in
the science of uniting the individual
consciousness with the ultimate
consciousness are different, but not the
educated, a person perfectly engaged
in even one, gains the result of both.

Conclusion – Both devotion and (sannyasin) renunciation right manner of living, but devotion like Mira Bai, where no pain and pleasure left in devotion, whatever left is love.

16- But of those whom this ignorance
has been destroyed by the knowledge of
the self; that knowledge is like the rising
sun illuminated by the ultimate truth.

Conclusion- In the sutra of Geeta, Shri Krishna again and again giving reference about wisdom and (sannyasin) renunciation, and he explained it. In presence of intelligence how ignorance disappears.

19- Those whose minds are situated in
equanimity, they conquer this world in
this very life; since they are endowed
with the equal vision of the ultimate
truth and free from all dualities, they
are situated in the ultimate truth.

Conclusion – whose mind is equipoise, he already has earned the liberty and happiness.

20, 21- Fully situated in the ultimate
truth, equipoise in spiritual intelligence,
devoid of delusion; one realized in
the ultimate truth neither rejoices
obtaining the pleasurable nor laments
when obtaining the unpleasurable.

One whose mind is not attached
to external sense objects enjoys the
happiness of the inner self; self-realized
in the ultimate truth by the science of
uniting the individual consciousness
with the ultimate consciousness,
one enjoys unlimited bliss.

Conclusion – Again, this sutra is giving same reference, being equipoise is the key of the happiness, calm, and freedom, this comes with (sannyasin) renunciation which is the path of wisdom. All happiness comes from your interior.

22, 23- O Arjuna, those pleasures
arising from the senses contacting

sense objects are indeed the source of
misery only; subject to a beginning
and an end; therefore, the spiritually
intelligent never take delight in them.

That person who is able to neutralize
in this life, the physical, mental and
emotional urges generated from desire and
passion, before the death of the body; he
is fully self-controlled and certainly happy.

Conclusion – Intelligent never totally involved in pain and pleasure, he always makes distance and do not totally attached to mundane things, his all effort toward balance life style.

24- One who experience internal
happiness with the mind immersed in
the self, and who sees the self within as
well; such a one perfecting the science of
uniting the individual consciousness with
the ultimate consciousness, spiritually
realizing the ultimate truth attains
the liberation of the ultimate truth.

Conclusion – This sutra is also giving same reference, introvert man, equipoise mind is key of all happiness and success and freedom.

25- Those seers of truth, whose doubts
have been dispelled, devoid of all sins,
engaged in self-realization and who

are always concerned for the spiritual
welfare of all living beings, achieve
liberation in the ultimate truth.

Conclusion – this sutra is also pointing toward same path. This is not different from above conclusion.

Ch-6, sh-1- Lord Krishna said: one who
enacts obligatory prescribed actions
without expectation of the result of
actions he is truly a renunciation and
a follower of the science of uniting
the individual consciousness with
the ultimate consciousness; not one
without prescribed duties, nor one who
merely renounces bodily activities.

Conclusion – (Sannyasin) renunciation does not at all mean renouncing mundane things, whosoever run away from his duties and become (sannyasi) recluse is deceiving himself.

2- O Arjuna, you should know that
which is acclaimed as renunciation is
the science of uniting the individual
consciousness with the ultimate
consciousness; since without renouncing
the desire for certain results one cannot
become perfected in the science of
uniting the individual consciousness
with the ultimate consciousness.

Conclusion – when in the shlok Shri Krishna said renounce, so he does not mean renouncing mundane things, he's simply mean understand renounce.

> 7, 8- The being who has conquered the
> mind, transcending the dualities of
> cold, heat, happiness, distress, honor
> and dishonor is firmly established with
> the ultimate consciousness within.

> One perfected in the science of uniting
> the individual consciousness with the
> ultimate consciousness by acquired
> Vedic knowledge and direct realization
> within the self, foxed in this state with
> senses fully controlled observing with
> equal vision a clod of dirt, a stone
> or gold is declared to be realized.

Conclusion – Your mind is the biggest enemy and best friend; whose mind is equipoise is a victor.

> 9- But more superior is one who with
> spiritual intelligence acts equally towards
> natural well-wishers, affectionate
> well-wishers, and enemies, those
> indifferent to disputes, mediators
> of disputes, the envious, friends,
> saintly person as well as the sinful.

Conclusion – Sannyasin, renunciation is above than all discrimination.

Ch-8, sh-11- That path which the learned knower of Vedic scriptures declares imperishable into which the great renounced ascetics devoid of sensual desires enters and that which striving to reach the vow of celibacy is maintained; I shall explain unto you in summation.

Conclusion – Sannyasin, renunciation is the most modern art of living.

Ch-13, Sh-2- Lord Krishna, said O Arjuna, the material body is known as the field of activity; those who know this describe those who know this as the knower of the field of activity.

Conclusion – Means Sannyasin, renunciation.

Ch-14, Sh-22,23,24,25- Lord Krishna said, one who feels no resentment at the appearance of illumination, activity as well as illusion, O Arjuna, nor desires their cessation; one who neutrally situated is not disturbed by the three modes of material nature, one who remains firmly poised without wavering knowing that the modes of material nature are the performer; One who is equipoise in happiness and distress, firmly situated internally, regarding equally a lump of earth, a stone of gold, equally disposed

towards the desirable and the undesirable,
in honor and dishonor, equal to both
friends and enemies, abandoning all
endeavors for activity and renunciation,
one is declared transcendental to the
three modes of material nature.

Conclusion – these sutras are not much different than above
shloks, balanced minded person is sannyasin, renunciation.

26- One who by the science of uniting the
individual consciousness with the ultimate
consciousness in pure loving devotion,
rendering unadulterated service exclusively
unto me; such a one completely
surmounts these three modes of material
nature and qualifies for elevation to the
realized platform of the ultimate truth.

Conclusion – controlled and equipoise mind.

Ch-16, Sh-1, 2, 3- Lord Krishna said,
the possessor of all opulence said;
fearless, pure heartedness, established in
the wisdom of discrimination of spirit
and matter by the science of uniting
the individual consciousness with the
ultimate consciousness, charity, self-
restraint, performance of sacrifice study
of Vedic scriptures, austerity, uprightness,
nonviolence, truthfulness, aversion to
fault finding, compassion to all being,

absence of avarice, gentleness, modesty
and determination. O Arjuna, Radiance,
forgiveness, fortitude, purity, freedom
from malice, absence of pride arises
in one born of the divine nature.

Conclusion – All the qualities comes with right lifestyle, and
the key to happiness and liberty is sannyasin, renunciation.

4- Pseudo-religiosity, pretentious pride,
conceitful arrogance, anger, harshness
and ignorance arise in one born of
the demoniac nature, O Arjuna.

Conclusion – Man has been keeping away from humanity
without the right knowledge and without sannyasin,
renunciation.

Ch-18, Sh-2- Lord Krishna, the possessor
of all opulence said, the leaned know
that abandonment of activities inspired
by certain desire is renunciation and
the experienced say relinquishing the
results of all actions is renunciation.

Conclusion – sacrifice the fruits of deed, when Lord Krishna
said sacrifice the fruit of a deed, so he means being equipoise
in interior. Once being balanced in the interior, so there is
no reason left worried about fruit of doing.

3, 4, 5, 6- Some in wisdom says to
renounce action, due to its defect of being

a desire and others say that actions based
on performance of sacrifice, charity and
austerity should not be renounced.
O Arjuna, hear from me, the factual understanding
regarding renunciation; verily renunciation is described as
threefold, O tiger among men.

Actions based on performance of
sacrifice, charity and austerity should
never be renounced; they certainly
must be enacted; performance of
sacrifice, charity and austerities are
purifying for those with wisdom.

Moreover, these activities should
be performed as duty, renouncing
attachment to certain results; this is my
topmost, definitive conclusion, O Arjuna.

Conclusion – renouncing is not a solution, but to
understanding it.

With time things change, once man
able to understand, what is worth doing
and what is not, and all these abilities
come with the right knowledge and all
the knowledge comes with most modern
art of living Sannyasin, renunciation.

7, 8, 9, 10- But renunciation of
prescribed activities is not recommended;

abandoning them due to illusion is declared as the nature of nescience.

Giving up such actions out of fear of bodily discomfort or as troublesome enacts renunciation in the nature of passion; one certainly never obtains the certain result of this renunciation.

O Arjuna, prescribed actions which are performed as a matter of duty giving up attachment to certain results is considered renunciation in the nature of goodness.

The intelligent renunciant endowed with the nature of goodness, freed from all doubts, neither disdains disagreeable actions nor becomes attached to agreeable ones.

Conclusion – Running away from your duties is not sannyasin, renunciation.

Intelligent never run away from his duties, because he knows the truth.

11-The embodied being can never completely give up activities; but it is described that by renouncing the certain results of actions that one is renounced.

Conclusion – renouncing mundane things is not possible, but understand them is possible, by which man can liberation from them.

> 22- That by which one is engrossed
> in some fragmental conception as if
> it encompasses all, irrational; without
> knowledge of reality and whimsically
> is called the nature of nescience.

Conclusion – Do not follow blindly anything, anybody or any religion, until you do not experience by yourself; do not defend anything without complete knowledge, this blindness, this incompletions of knowledge is the reason of man's misery, ignorance of the man is the reason of his failure and misery.

> 23- That action which is devoid of certain
> desires, free from attraction and repulsion,
> without attachment; which is performed
> as duty is called the nature of goodness.

Conclusion – work without desire is key to happiness, is key of liberation.

> 24- Then again that action which one
> with desires for certain result or one
> egotistical performs with great endeavor
> is known as in the nature of passion.

Conclusion – work of desire becomes the cause of pain and misery for man.

25- That action which is begun
out of illusion without considering
consequence, destruction, violence
and one's own ability to fulfill it is
called in the nature of nescience.

Conclusion –Ignorance about (Maya) illusory become misery of man.

26- The liberated and detached performer
or actions devoid of false ego, endued
with fortitude and great enthusiasm,
unaffected by success and failure is
called in the nature of goodness.

Conclusion – This sutra is giving reference of above shlok, as I revealed above, desire-less deed is key of most modern art of living sannyasin, renunciation. This is the key of happiness and success of man.

27- The obsessed craving certain desires,
desires, greedy, malevolent, impure,
subject to joy and sorrow, such a performer
is declared in the nature of passion.

Conclusion – as I said before, who is totally involved, totally lost in illusion (Maya) has to suffer pain his whole life.

28- The unqualified, degraded, slothful,
deceptive, overbearing, lazy, morose and
procrastinating performer of actions
is called in the nature of ignorance.

Conclusion – this sutra's conclusion is same as above; he who totally involves in Maya, illusion has to suffer.

> 29, 30, 31, 32- Hear this, O Arjuna,
> I shall now describe comprehensively
> and individually the spiritual
> intelligence as well as the resolve
> according to the threefold variety
> of the modes of material nature.
>
> O Arjuna, spiritual intelligence in
> the nature of goodness is that which
> factually knows the propriety of
> things as well as the impropriety of
> things, duty and non-duty, fear and
> fearlessness, bondage and liberation.
>
> That spiritual intelligence, O
> Arjuna by which righteousness
> and unrighteousness; what is duty
> and what is non-duty are perceived
> imperfectly is in the nature of passion.
>
> That spiritual intelligence enveloped in
> ignorance, which regards righteousness
> as righteousness and everything
> contrary to what they are, is in the
> nature of nescience, O Arjuna.

Conclusion – the ignorant man, misguided man spreads chaos in the society, and when chaos spread in the society, so whole world be scattered.

33- O Arjuna, the uninterrupted,
determination which motivates the
activities of the mind, the life breath
and the senses by the science of
uniting the individual consciousness
with the ultimate consciousness is
determination of the nature of goodness.

Conclusion – balanced mind is on the path of Sannyasin, renunciation.

34- But that determination by which
righteousness, sensual desire and
wealth are motivated by attachment
to certain desires, O Arjuna, is
in the nature of passion.

Conclusion – imbalanced mind cannot become sannyasin, recluse.

35- That Determination O Arjuna
by which the unintelligent is unable
to abandon dreaming, fearing,
grieving, depression and foolhardiness
is in the nature of science.

Conclusion – unintelligent has to suffer in vain.

36, 37- O Arjuna, but now hear from
me, the three kinds of happiness by the
cultivation of which one enjoys and one
attains the cessation of all distress. That

which in the beginning is like poison and
at the end is like nectar. That happiness
arising from the serenity of spiritual
intelligence of the embodied self is
designated in the nature of goodness.

Conclusion – New is always quite hard to accept, digest in starting. Once it would be accepted it could bring great changes.

38, 39- That happiness forms the
combination of the senses and the sense
objects which in the beginning is like
nectar and at the end is like poison; that
is known as in the nature of passion.

Happiness arising from sleep, sloth
and irresponsibility which deludes the
embodied self in the beginning and at the
end is called in the nature of nescience.

Conclusion – Sooner or later unintelligent, the fool has to suffer.

49, 50, 51, 52, 53- Detached by spiritual
intelligence from everything, controlling
the mind, without material desires, one
attains the paramount perfection in the
cessation of reactions by renunciation.

Now hear in summation from me,
O Arjuna, how one achieving the

perfection of cessation of reactions
attains the supreme state of knowledge.

Endowed with spiritual intelligence,
fully purified an regulating the self by
determination, giving up mundane
sense objects such as hearing and
touching and casting away obsession
and repulsion, avoidance of materialistic
persons, moderate in eating, controlled
in body, mind and speech, always
absorbed in the science of yoga,
detached from all mundane things, the
relinquishing of egotism, power, pride,
lust, anger and accepting charity and
donations; the peaceful one without
any sense of proprietorship is qualified
for realizing the ultimate truth.

Conclusion – Sannysin (renunciation) is the modern than modern art of living, this is requirement of today, without sannyasin this society and this world would not stand long, there is only way to escape from man's all problems, all misery, and this society has to accept this new art of living, Sannyasin (renunciation).

Renunciation (Sannyasin) is intelligence and freedom, renunciation (sannyasin) purifies body and soul, and it purifies interiority and exteriority, sanniyasin purifies man's whole being.

The Sculpture worship

Ch-9, Sh-23-O Arjuna, those who
worship devotedly different demigods,
although faithfully; they also worship me
only; but in an unauthorized manner.

Sculpture worship was great discovery; this was not an ordinary discovery in human history, but with time its original meaning has lost, and with time, this was just left superstition and part of rituals, there is no depth left in this ritual in this worship, these are just hollow rituals, because man has forgotten its real meaning, people who believe that they are modern, intelligent, and not superstition.

But they are not enough modern and intelligent to understand sculpture worship, to understand Sanatana religion and its deeper meaning, they are living with Sanatana religion superficially, their intelligence is not enough which take them in the deep sense of Sculpture worship, man has to become real modern, man has to renounce to old thoughts and adopt new thought, new vision,

How idolatry, Sculpture worship is a great discovery?

When one worships God, he requires a medium, without sculpture, without this medium would not be able to focus on worship, their eyes would move one place to another, by sink in this sculpture man can achieve a higher state of conscious, one can achieve a higher state of awakening, sculpture worship is not ordinary invention, it has really great meaning.

you cannot be able to meditate in the empty room, just one sculpture make you able to concentrate and disconnect you from outside world, but without statue your imagination will run faster than your imagination, it would be so difficult for you to hold it, but with only one statue you can meditate, you can concentrate, focus and disconnect with all other thoughts, this is the right and great way to immerse in devotion, in ancient time our elders discover this invention, flowers and its mala make our mind relax and other worship things like fragrance it's all for our mind relaxation, this the way to calm your brain and relax yourself, and make it comfortable and create beautiful atmosphere around you, but with time many superstitions have taken place and real meaning has lost, and idolatry has become totally useless.

The awakening

Chapter -2, Shlok-38

sukha-duhkhe same krtva labhalabhau jayajayau
tato yuddhaya yujyasva naivam papam avapsyasi

Being equipoised in happiness
and unhappiness, profit and
loss, victory and defeat;

Thereafter do battle for battle and in this
way you will not incur sinful reaction

Awakening is the state in which man becomes conscious, consciousness of your interiority, consciousness of your being, many possibilities opens for conscious man.

This is not the only life; there is life after life, every living creature transform into another life. But your life will good or better or bad or worse, it all depends, how you are living this life,

When Shri Krishna says being equipoised in happiness and unhappiness, profit and loss, if you will be equipoise in all conditions in all situations, you will not bond with any sin, you will not bond with any karma, deed. In this way you will become precious if you take birth so it would be a great birth, you will have born as real King.

But the man's story is totally different,

Man and Technologies

Man has lived his life with full of misery, wherever you take a look you will find man's misery, the misery has no ending, to remove this misery, to get rid of this pain, to get rid of this problem, to get rid of this,

The man has spent his whole life and use his all efforts for the solutions, but man is not able to get rid of these problems, he couldn't come over to this misery, the misery stood still, the man had done a lot of invention, lot of discovery because of this,

Man has always been finding a way out from this pain, but the pain is growing with time, generation to generation, man has tried to rid of these problems in wrong direction,

This is man's nature, not to stop just keep trying, but he is trying on the wrong side, he is going toward to darkness, he is going to downward,

Man's all effort is happening on the wrong side, but after all this man couldn't come over from this misery, man is very blockhead, he does not know surrender if he sticks with his arrogance so he would stay blockhead, that is the reason of his unhappy life.

He is still living his life with lots of conditions, whether he is rich or poor, rich and poor both are living their life in misery,

Man did not accept yet that his all discovery, his all invention has a limit, he will be staying limited with his all discovery and machines, but somewhere inside his deep introvert, he knows that this is not the right path, which he has chosen.

Because after creating all these equipment, all these machines, all these weapons all these technologies, he could not find the solution,

His condition is getting worse than before, his all discovery, his all invention could not take him away from his problems, instead of taking him away, all man's discovery is man's arrangement to take him to the graveyard,

Instead of this all these technologies pushing him to the graveyard to the hell, all these technologies have made to man slave, man cannot do anything with his wish, his all freedom has gone, all the technologies made name of man to give him freedom, to give him liberty, to give him comfort, for his happiness, to give him power, but power has gone to the wrong hands, very few people have all the power, and those have the power, they are treating people like slave, they are taking decision for us, so what has left in the end for man just slavery, just pain, all this border and war, slavery, riot, hate, more poor people, more hungry people, more competition, more difficulties, things become worse, instead of happiness, beauty, comforts, fragrance, man has no future ahead, man is going toward war, toward riot, and toward pain. He is going toward to destruction. Man needs the right solution and the solution will come from the Geeta's sutras for man's liberation and happiness,

"The solution is Sannyasin, the solution is Geeta's sutras,

Being equipoised in happiness and unhappiness, profit and loss, victory and defeat; this is the sutra of Sannyasin, man's all machines, all invention, cannot give man happiness, man-made machinery has given pain and misery and created problems, become the reason for destruction, but this formula, this Sutra of Geeta will give man utter happiness, utter joy, and give man liberty from all the pain and problems.

If man disconnect from this Maya, from this illusion, and understand illusion, (Maya) man can get, what he should have got,

When saints talk about Maya, illusion, people think about renouncing worldly, mundane things, and live their life in saint Ashram, because our saints tell renouncing mundane things, but this is not the true definition of Maya when this sutra's real meaning will reveal that this sutra will not only bring utter joy in man's life, but also this sutra will make man supreme being. Awaken man's whole hidden potential, to make use of this sutra, man has to understand this sutra, people have read and cram Geeta's all sutra, but did not understand real meaning, this is why I have explaining and revelation its sutras, its Shloks, being equipoised in happiness and unhappiness, profit and loss, victory and defeat; man's mind is playful, which does not allow man to be equipoise, this is the whole problem's subtle cause, man's playful mind is the reason, it is not easy to overcome this mind, but with practice and time man can be able to overcome from this, man can achieve peace mind, true happiness, and true joy.

Man's mind tells him, what is his and what is not, it divides man one from another, all sensitivity of man, all emotions, all relations is because of mind, mind is the cause of all the mundane things,

When man will understand his mind, his whole point of views, his attitude, his whole society, his whole life will totally change, this will bring balance to man's mind and in his life.

But this is not happening in this way, man's actions are totally different, but with intelligence he would change,

Man is too sensitive for one and insensitive for another, this sutra can bring great balance and incorruptibility in this society, in this world,

This imbalance or your mind is the reason for your all pain and misery, that is why Shri Krishna has given this Sutra to keep the man away from pain and misery, loss and defeat,

I have heard, many people saying that I do help other people, our life is dedicated to needy people, we do not live for ourselves, but for the society, we do not care about our happiness,

You also must have heard those people saying that we are doing this for you because I want to you see happy,

People give their food to other, people feed other people, and people help another,

One day Bhakta, who lives in my neighborhood, he said, I do not understand, how can anyone be so insensitive, unemotional, I cannot see other people unhappy, I cannot see people hungry, and he always helps people, sometimes give them food, give them clothes, and help people all the way he can.

He was telling me, Satti I cannot see anybody in pain, it really hurts me, it is very difficult for me to see anybody in pain, I asked him, you help people because you cannot see their pain, you feel their pain, this is why you always ready to help people, he replied yes,

There is a subtle reason behind this, man has to dig it to reveal this subtle reason, when a man helps others, actually he did all for himself, in subtle he really does not care about others, it's all for him.

So I reply Bhakta, you do not help others you help yourself, whatever you do, you do because you are very sensitive person, emotional person, this is why whenever you see anybody suffering, you felt bad for them, your eyes get wet, so whatever you do for needy, you do not do for others, he said no, I do for others, those in need, I said, no it is all for you, you really do not care about others, you cannot bear that much pain, this the reason, he said, I care about others, that is why I do help them, I said, you help them because you wanted to help yourself, you feeling uncomfortable, you are feeling pain, by doing this you feel comfortable, you feel good, feel happy,

he was totally disagreed, he does not want to understand what I try to tell him, because his ego got hurt to heard this, he was not agreed with me, he was repeating that I help people, not for myself, I help them for their happiness, yes it feels good when I did this, I replied, yes this is my point, people who are sensitive and those help others and feel good, they actually doing this because this their nature, and you too do for yourself, not for others,

There is the subtle nature of man, whatever he does, he does for himself, so he who is emotional and emotionless both are equal, there is not much different between both kind of people, just their actions are different to each other, opposite to each other, but the reason in subtle is same. They both do this for their happiness.

Who he is sensitive, emotional and who he is insensitive, emotionless, both are equal, there is not much different between both of them, one need to change the point of view to see them.

Sensitive help needy because he cannot see them in pain, he feels unhappy, so he helps others to make himself happy, as he helps others his mind overcomes from pain, and the person who is insensitive, not helpful, does not help because he does not feel bad, he does not feel pain, to watch needy people pain, so he does not help others. It is man's mind who is playing the game, this is why man has to balance his mind to control things, and otherwise he will be a puppet of mind.

I am not saying that helping others is not good, but I'm trying to help man to understand his own mind, if the man will understand and keep a sharp eye on his mind so his life will totally change, his life will become utterly happy and joyful. The conscious mind is awakening mind; conscious mind is peace mind.

If there were any medicine, after take that medicine insensitive person becomes sensitive and sensitive become insensitive, so you will be shocked to see this that they both will differ, their action will be different,

So man is good or bad it all depend on this that what category mind man has, sensitive and insensitive.

This story does not say that do not help people, it means man's mind is very playful, this is sublet that create many plays in his life, which keeps man in the suffering, this mind's playfulness is the reason of man's misery, man's all problems, but if you understand this sutra. Being equipoised in happiness and unhappiness, profit and loss, victory and defeat;

Man does not need to change his life, his work, his life will be same, but he will be utterly happy if he will understand this sutra, his mind will totally change, after being involved in all the activities, man will untouched from all the mundane things, and his life will become utterly happy, man's all relationships, man's all activities, it is nothing but memory imprint of mind, if this imprint will change so your mother, you sister, your brother, your father, your all friends, you all relatives are not your relatives, these all relations, are your memory imprint, if this imprint changes so no relationship will evade, man born with this nature, sensitive or insensitive, it is all in his gene, in his DNA.

If man understands this sutra, so he will not be insensitive as he is now, but he will become balanced person, this is sutra of intelligence, which remove discrimination from the society, man will be equal to each other, with this sutra, his family but whole society will become his family, so this sutra has the greatest possibilities to change the man and the world.

If this world accepts and understand Geeta's sutras, so how this world could change, man cannot even imagine,

Being equipoised in happiness and unhappiness, profit and loss, victory and defeat; this Shlok not only bring utter happiness also this sutra can make the man powerful, awaken his whole Chakras, awaken his Kundaliny Power, the power would not bring destruction but brings utter joy, utter happiness. This Kundalini awakening will bring great power with it if this will awaken man really does not need any machine.

The blueprint of Kundalini awakening.

The theory starts from here, once you understand the theory of fate, after this you can understand what I try to explain here, because without intelligence you cannot awaken Kundalini, once you understand theory of fate completely, then you need place where you can meditate and nobody would disturb you, this process can take month or more, it depends on your state, the theory of Kundalini awaken is very simple and easy, one does not have to do anything, whatever will happen it would happen in your interior,

When you sit on meditation so lots of thought will come into your mind, you just let them flow in your mind, you do not need to stop or attach with them, you just have to think and focus on one thing, which is first step you are nothing, there is nothing that you can do, even your thought are not in your control, you have to think this with deep of your mind that you are not doer, you are not watcher, there is nothing in this whole existence that you can do, whatever happens, happens by itself, it is chain reaction, your whole being is chain reaction's action, you just have to stop your mind, once your mind agree with this it will totally stop and go to unconsciousness state, once it would be unconscious.

As your mind totally disappear so your whole being will awaken, your Kundalini will awaken, you will awaken, you will completely detach of Maya Illusion, once this will happen so you would be able to do anything, you can create a new universe, whatever you want to do you can do, you will know that you are God, there is no other God, you are sleeping God, the God is unconscious yet, who does not know about himself.

Kundalini awakening's rule is not to leave and not to hold, balance between holdings and leaving, it all happens in your mind, when one makes this great balance between and holding and leaving, so his Kundalini awakens.

Ch-2, Sh-52, 53, 55, 56, 57, 58, 60- When
your spiritual intelligence overcomes this

myriad of delusion at that time you will
become indifferent towards all that has
been heard and all that is to be heard.

When your spiritual intelligence,
unaffected and uninfluenced by karmic
interpretations of the Vedas remains
steady; at that time, you will achieve
the pure spiritual state of the science of
uniting the individual consciousness
with the ultimate consciousness.

One whose mind is undisturbed by
distress, without desires for happiness, free
from attachment, fear and anger; that sage
is known as steadfast in consciousness.

One who without attachment in every
respect, neither rejoices nor curses
obtaining correspondingly good or evil;
he is established in perfect knowledge.

When one completely withdraws the
sense similarly as the tortoise withdraws
its limbs, from the object of the sense
he is established in perfect knowledge.

O Arjuna the senses are so turbulent they
can forcibly lead astray the mind of even
a vigilant person of sound judgment.

Conclusion – whosoever controlled his senses can have controlled anything, that person is victor, the sutra has been revealed in Geeta's Shlok, being equipoise in your interior, once man equipoises interiorly, he awakens his whole being potential and this potential awakens by intelligence. But man's mind is very clever and habitual of its old habits, it will cheat you without your conscious.

> 61- Keeping under control all the sense,
> the self-controlled should meditate
> on me; since for one whose sense
> have been brought under control is
> established in perfect knowledge.

Conclusion - When you being equipoise your Kundalini awakens and when Kundalini awakens your total potential awaken, you totally awake.

> 62, 63, 67- While concentrating
> on objects of the senses a person
> develops attachment to the sense
> object; from attachment desires are
> born, from desire anger arises.

> From anger delusion occurs, from
> delusion bewilderment of memory,
> after forgetfulness of memory the loss
> of spiritual intelligence and losing
> spiritual intelligence one perishes.

> "Whichever" among the various
> senses the wandering mind becomes

> engrossed in that sense certainly leads
> astray his intelligence like the wind
> snatches away a boat on the water.

Conclusion – Human mind is subtle, it is very hard to control it, one has to keep the sharp eye on it, just a little misstep, a small error and you will come in the clutches of your mind, so a man has to keep remembering himself.

> 64- But that self-controlled being who
> follows the Vedic injunctions whole
> amidst objects of the senses, freed from
> attachment and aversion, with senses
> governed by the self; attains the precious
> mercy of the ultimate personality.

Conclusion – The balanced mind gets God's grace.
With all the shloks Lord Krishna is referring to the same point, Sanniyasin and equipoise person get God's grace.

> 70, 71, 72- The sage achieves the peace
> that is approaching all kinds of enjoyable
> sense objects remains unaffected; like
> unto the ocean being always being
> filled by approaching rivers and not that
> person desirous of sense enjoyment.

> That person attains peace, who giving up
> all material desires for sense gratification
> lives free from attachment, free from
> false ego and sense of proprietorship.

O Arjuna, having gained the realization
of the ultimate truth, one is never again
deluded and even at the moment of death,
being situated in this state, liberation from
the material existence and attainment of
the ultimate consciousness is assured.

Conclusion - When you will understand (Maya) an illusion so there is no possible way left by which you would make stop, yours Kundalini will awaken, and you will become super human. The man has to accept most art of living and being equipoise.

Ch-3, Sh-18, 19, 20, -

In this world for him no purpose is
gained by discharge by of actions neither
is any sin incurred by non-discharge
of actions and among all living beings
never needs to depend upon anyone.

Therefore, without attachment, without
interruption, perfectly perform prescribed
actions; since by performing prescribed
actions a person achieves the highest *good*.
By performing prescribed activities King Janaka and
others certainly realized complete perfection; likewise,
you should perform as well considering for the sake of
benefiting the welfare of the world.

Conclusion – Just proceed your duties without misguided. There is no bond and duties left for an equipoised man.

He gets totally free, get totally liberate from all his deeds and its fruits.

21, 22, 23, 24, 25, 28, 33- Whichever
and however, a great personality conducts
him common men do also; whatever he
accepts as authority that and that alone
certainly the entire world will follow.

O Arjuna, in the spiritual worlds,
the heavenly worlds and the material
worlds there is no prescribed duty
for me; neither I have the lack of
anything nor is required; yet still I
am engaged in prescribed activities.

O Arjuna, if ever I would not engage in
prescribed activities certainly all men
would follow my path in all respects.

If I cease to perform prescribed actions
the inhabitants of all the worlds would
be put into ruin and I would be the
cause of undesirable population and
would destroy all these living entities.

O Arjuna, just as the ignorant act
attached to activities; even so the wise
being unattached should act desiring
to benefit the welfare of the world.

But O mighty-armed one, a knower
of the truth does not require certain
actions, there is no cause required
to be left for certain actions, and he
does not need to depend on others.

Even a knowledgeable person acts
according to his own nature; all living
entities are controlled by their own
natures. What can repression accomplish?

Conclusion – Intelligence man always set an example for others; every intelligent man has a same truth, but their words, language can be different, but the deep meaning would be the same because the truth is always one, the way of explaining things can be different but truth cannot change. (Sannyasi) Recluse also involve in mundane things, but they never attach to them.

Ch-4, Sh-17, 18, 19, 20, 21, 22, 23-
The subject of actions prescribed in
the Vedas should be understood, the
subject of actions prohibited in the Veda
should be understood and the subject of
renunciation of action as prescribed by the
Vedas should be understood; because the
intricacies of actions are very mysterious.

One who realizes the renunciation
of action in activities and action in
the renunciation of activities, he
is the spiritual intelligence among

mankind, transcendentally situated
a perfect performer of all actions.

One whose every undertaking is
devoid of motivation for certain desires
and sense gratification and who has
incinerated all activities in the fire
of pure knowledge; the spiritually
intelligent describe him as educated.

After giving up attachment to certain
results, always satisfied, indifferent
to external phenomena; he in
spite of being engaged in activities
does not do anything at all.

Bereft of desire, controlled in mind
and body, relinquishing all conceptions
of proprietorship, that person never
incurs sinful reaction performing only
actions to maintain body sustenance.

Satisfied with whatever comes of its
own accord, tolerant of dualities,
devoid of envy to others and whole
performing is equipoise in the
success or failure is never affected.

For one who is unattached to material
nature, who is liberated, whose heart is
situated in transcendence, who performs

all actions as the sacrifice into the ultimate
personality, all reactions are dissolved.

Conclusion – This is very hard to know what should man
do and what should not do, man needs right guidance and
the Geeta is the source of this right knowledge. He who does
not follow the old and rotten path. He who simply focuses,
who keep involve in all activities without any greed. Just
flow with the wave, this is the right manner of living.

Ch-5, Sh-8, 9, 11, 13, 18, 26, 27, 28- A
performer of prescribed activities, a
knower of truth, having ascertained that
is the senses engaged in their various
sense objects, never thinks he is doing
anything; in spite of seeing, hearing,
touching, smelling, eating, moving,
sleeping, breathing, speaking, excreting
and grasping; like the involuntary
opening and closing of the eyelids.

Followers of the science of uniting the
individual consciousness with the ultimate
consciousness, giving up attachment
perform prescribed actions by the body,
by the mind, by the intelligence, and by
the separated senses for purifying the self.

Mentally renouncing all certain activities,
the self-controlled embodied being within
the physical body of nine opening; free
from thinking he is the actual doer of

anything and free from thinking he is
the cause of anything resides happily.

Only those who see with equal vision the
ultimate truth in a Brahman endowed
with Vedic knowledge and humanity,
in a cow, in an elephant, in a dog and
in the lower animal eating members of
humanity are learned in genuine wisdom.

For those renounced, who aware
of the soul are self-realized and
who are free from lust and anger;
liberation in the ultimate truth
occurs in this life and the next.

Conclusion – Intelligent neither attach nor detach with anything he stays balanced inside himself, one who is intelligent never discriminates, he always sees with equal eyes.

Ch-6, Sh-5, 6, 11, 12, 32, The
conditioned being must be delivered from
the material nature of the realized mind.
The conditioned being must not become
degraded; since this very mind is the
friend of the conditioned being as well
as the enemy of the conditioned being.

For the being who has conquered
the mind; that being mind is the
best of friends, but for one whose

mind is uncontrolled, that very mind
acts as the worst of enemies.

In a sacred and purified place after
establishing a set neither too high
nor too low of kusa grass, deerskin or
natural cloth; thereupon sitting firmly
on that seat, controlling the mind and
activities of the senses making the mind
one-pointed; one in realization should
meditate by the science of uniting the
individual consciousness with the ultimate
consciousness for purifying the mind.

32, One who perceives in comparison
with the self, all living entities equally,
in happiness and distress; such a one
perfected in the science of uniting the
individual consciousness with the ultimate
consciousness is considered the highest.

Conclusion - Mind is both enemy and friend of man,
one need to have a very brave heart to become a (sannyasi)
recluse, with this one become interiorly happy. Determine
your mind and take a strong decision then (sannyasin)
renunciation will happen with you, but with company of
society (Sannyasin) renunciation will become easier, with
right practice man can control his mind, learn by others
mistake, whosoever has this ability can possibly become
(sannyasi) recluse.

Ch-7, Sh-3, Out of many thousands
of men hardly one endeavor for the
perfection of self-realization, and of those
so endeavoring hardly one has achieved
the perfection of self-realization and of
those hardly one knows me in truth.

Conclusion – The victor is the chosen one. Whether he is victor or loser either bonded with fate.

Ch-8, Sh-3, Lord Krishna said, the
supreme indestructible reality has declared
the ultimate truth. Its eternal nature is the
embodied self. Procreation and the desired
development in the material existence of
the physical bodies of all living entities
are delineated as certain action.

12, Withdrawing from sense objects all
the senses of the body and steadying
the mind within the heart, fixed in self-
realization with the life breath in the head
is being established perfectly in the science
of uniting the individual consciousness
with the ultimate consciousness.

Conclusion – Wisdom, Intelligence is indestructible, wisdom will always alive, before and after this existence, with meditation and Yoga one can awaken his intelligence.

Ch-9, Sh-20, 28, 31- Knower of the
prescribed rituals of the three Vedas,

purified of sins by remnants of the
heavenly elixir, worship me indirectly
by such offerings of sacrifice to the
demigods; they aspire for entry to
the heavenly spheres, where after
reaching as their reward the world
of Indra, enjoy the celestial pleasures
of the demigods in heaven.
In this way you will become free from auspicious and
inauspicious reactions from the bondage of actions;
having fixed the mind in renunciation by the science of
uniting the individual consciousness with the ultimate
consciousness, being so endowed you will proceed
into me.
One swiftly becomes endowed with righteousness and
justly obtains everlasting peace. O Arjuna declares it
boldly, my devotee never perishes.

Conclusion – This life is not only life, according to this life
next life takes shape, the all the atmosphere, the parents,
siblings, friends, relatives everything whatever happens, it is
all because of your past life, past life of man is controlling
this life, man does not have any control on this life, but he
still uselessly in proud that he is the reason of happening
events. The man is not a doer, he has to accept this.

Ch-12, Sh-10, 11, 12- And if in the
practice of reminding me, you are
also unfit then become dedicated
to the performance of duties for me

and in performing activities for my
satisfaction you will achieve perfection.
And if also this you are unable to perform then taking
shelter with me by the science of uniting the individual
consciousness with the ultimate consciousness, controlling
the mind perform all activities renouncing the results.
Knowledge is superior to practice, meditation is
considered better than knowledge; renouncing the results
of actions than meditation, verily by such renunciation
comes tranquility.

Conclusion –Become devotee, if devotion is not your way, become (sannyasi) recluse, if you cannot become a (sannysi) recluse, understand what is renouncing, if this is also difficult for you, try to be balanced.

Ch-18, Sh-54- Being one with the
ultimate truth, joyous within the
self, neither laminating nor craving;
equipoise to all living entities, one
achieves transcendental devotion to me.

Conclusion – The whole lesson referring about (sannysin) renunciation, being equipoise, intelligence and unintelligent. In this way, he who tries to get the result according to that.

Who is God

Chapter-10, Shlok-8

aham sarvasya prabhavo mattah sarvam pravartate

iti matva bhajante mam budha bhava-samanvitah

I am the original generating cause of all causes, everything emanates from me;

Comprehending this spiritually intelligent endowed with devotional sentiments become devoted into me.

If you tell this sutra to any Hindu, he would agree with this sutra and he will not put up any question, but everyone is not same, not everyone will agree with this sutra, those have curiosity surely those people will want to know, how Lord Krishna is the original generating cause of all causes,

I don't have any proof to prove this Shloka, but I have a theory, I can explain this with my experience, what I have experienced, I can only reveal in front of you, first man has to understand, who is the God? What is the God? If the man's definition of God is a fiction character, someone who has the power is the God, so this is the different thing, but my experience is about God is totally different from this definition, my experience says,

God is awakening, whosoever awakens becomes the God, this the only definition of God.

And God is nothing else but an awakening, become the reason of all generating causes. And what is awakening? When I say awakening so I mean, awakening of man, when man's being awaken, so he becomes God,

God is just awakening; God is just consciousness, when the man awakens, when man become conscious so he becomes God, God is nothing else but an awakening, whosoever awakens becomes god, this is the only definition of God.

Man did never taste of consciousness, taste of awakening, so when a man will taste of consciousness, man will know the beauty of God, the beauty of awakening, beauty of consciousness, it all comes from interior of man, the taste of freedom and the fragrance, the joy and the happiness,

God is awakening except this, there is no other definition of God, everything man has done to persuade God is irrelevant, meaningless, the only thing can persuade to God is your consciousness, but man sees God in temples, churches, Masque, Girjaghar, Gurudwara, people who believe that God lives in these places, so they are living in misconception, and man's all prayers are irrelevant, man cannot find any God by cramming words, no man can meet his God, God is not man whom you will persuade, God is wisdom, God is intelligence, so to understand God, you have to be intelligence, you have to awaken your wisdom your inner intelligence, otherwise there is no other way to know the God, to know the Krishan, to know this Geeta's sutra. Without this wisdom without this intelligence man's life will stay empty,

But the wrong thing is that the religion's teachers have many ways to drag man to into temples, Churches, Girjaghar, Masque. There is no problem going to the Temple, church, and Masque, but the problem is blindly following somebody or something, without knowing that this is right or wrong, what is the reason behind this, from where all these starts, and what is its purpose. Following religion is like drug, religion is man's shackle, man is narrow-minded, this is why he is not able to free from it, religion made to spread happiness in man's life,

But in the present time these religions are doing something else, religion is dividing man, one to another, man does not understand, what is happening with his society, with him, with this world,

All the system has changed, corrupted, the religious teachers have given drugs of greed to man, and man blindly follows these religious teachers, man is very greedy, this is why man's greed doesn't allow a man to ask the question and choose another way, the way of freedom, man does not have much dared to choose his own path, one need the great dare to choose his own path, because the different and new is always difficult, because it is different and new.

Man always makes the ways of shortcuts, but with short cuts originality lost, so religion's originality has lost, just hollow body has left, no soul in these religions,

The worse thing is this that this path keeps man unconscious, as long as man stays in this condition, man's possibility to know the truth and awaken himself from deep sleep, has been faded, because of all superstitious, man has taught from his birth, all these superstitious has bond man in its clutch, man has become very weak to escape from those superstitious, the only thing can set man free is (Sannyasin) renunciation, man has to accept the truth, and accepting truth is not easy, because, man's believe is very much old and become strong, taught and told by his parents and so called religion teacher,

Man's mind has been faded, this is why his soul also has been faded, that is why man has this worse nature, he kills, he lies, he cheats, he jealous, the all worse thing can happen with man, is happening with him, man need freedom, man need medicine and his medicine is Meditation, Sannyasin, renunciation, calm, freedom, beauty, until man will not get his medicine of truth, he will remain sick, man's soul is suffering, his mind is also suffering, he will unaware from truth.

And this unawareness is cause of all the problems, become aware, become conscious and life great and awesome life. Because man deserve to live this kind of life, now all up to man what he chooses, complete freedom and complete happiness or his old prison and painful life.

But there is fear that does not allow the man to be liberated from Maya, an illusion.

Revelation of Fear

It is fear of man, which does not allow a man to awaken, he is still unconscious, he is in a deep sleep because this is fear of man, which keeps the man in its grip.

Until a man does not face his fear, he would not be able to liberate of his deep sleep, of unconsciousness. The soul, the inner core of the man is suffering. The man has the fear of (Maya) illusion, he does not want to hear about the truth, about the Illusion, Maya. The attraction of the Maya, the illusion is so strong man does not want to leave this,

Because man has made lots of dreams so how can he break these dream and renounce them, this is very hard to believe that whatever he dreams about, he lives for it, for Maya, he is getting mad without any reason.

He is so busy with his life, in his dreams, these dreams have caught man for thousands of years, it has totally entered in his veins, in his blood, in his gene (DNA). It will take some time to get free from this, this is difficult but with right education man will get free from his fear.

The man is living his life in the middle and this middle thing is keeping man incomplete, keeping man unconscious Keeping man unawakened. The man has ignored to spirituality, man lives as materialistic, he has a great fear to accept the truth.

Fear of man is the massive problem, but it does not mean that he should fight with this, he does not need to fight with it, fighting with fear is not the answer, the fight makes the problem unsolved.

There is a story from ancient time, there was a (Rakshasa) Monster, he was very powerful, no warrior could defeat him, one day a great warrior had encountered with that

(Rakshasa) Monster, the warrior fighting with the Rakshasa Monster for many days but he could not defeat him, he was the great warrior, he has great potentials, he had beaten many Rakshasa Monster before, but he was not able to beat him, but the Rakshasa Monster was getting stronger day by day, the warrior has used his all skill, but the Rakshasa Monster taking over the warrior, at last warrior has accepted his defeat and he left the battle field, and the Rakshasa Monster had seizure whole town and oppressed the citizens of town, nobody dare to stand against him, the Rakshasa Monster was destroying the down, destroying the food.

Seeing this condition God has to interfere in this situation, God has to come in reincarnation, and he challenged the Monster Rakshasa and in the battle field they fought and without using his power God defeat the Rakshasa Monster in few hours, when he came back to town the warrior asked him, how did you beat the Rakshasa Monster without using your powers, God replied that when you were fighting, there was great anger in you and the anger become Rakshasa's Monster's food and by your anger, he was getting stronger and stronger, this is why you did not defeat him, and when I fought with the Monster Rakshasa there was no anger in me, and he did not get power from me and his power come to an end and when his power totally finished so he finished.

And now how anger is related to fear, actually fear is very much related to anger, when one gets anger there is always a reason behind the anger, in this story warrior wants to defeat Monster, because he wants to defeat so he was worried about this he had fear that maybe he would not defeat Rakshasa Monster, he might be lost to him, this is why he was getting too much involve in the fight and with the boiled blood, he was fighting because in sublet, warrior knows that Monster can defeat him this fear was trying to take him over, this fear is totally griped him and because of this fear he was fighting with more passion and more anger and this was the reason, he would not able to defeat Monster.

Man is not only fearful he is also in confusion, and this confusion spread by man himself,

In the history of man, whatever has happened good or evil, there is a big reason behind all this happening, and the man is the reason of all the reason. Man commits crime because of his fear, he steals, he cheats, he lies, he kills. The cause of all these things is the fear of man, because of fear, man hates to each other.

Behind of all the competitions reason is the same, there is a massive list of man's fear, which does not seem to end anywhere. Because man is so much worried about his possession, the possession he has or the possession he wants to achieve, he does not want to lose anything, he has fear that if he would not speak lie so he would not get what he wants, whether it is money, relationship, possession, there is lots of reason of man's fear.

The man has made barriers and borders, man has divided man from man, the cause of all his sickness is the fear, he has to aware about his sickness, otherwise things would not change.

The man has to meet his fear for the solution of it until he would not accept his fear, this sickness this fear keeps the man in his fear. Once man will catch on of his fear then his life will completely change, man need right guidance to come over of this fear, the right guidance the right knowledge will come, once he surrenders to himself to sannyasin, renunciation, if he accepts Sannyasin, renunciation, so he gets the solution of his problems, all the question's answer is sannyasin, renunciation, when man will accept this (Sannyasin) renunciation, the most modern manner of living his all the problems will solve, with the intelligence, manner of living no fear spare in his life, all the fear will go.

Fear comes from exteriority until man will be living extrovert life fear will stand still, but with (Sannyasin) renunciation all the fear will disappear, because (sannyasi) recluse lives introvert life and (Sannyasin) renunciation get totally pure your introvert and when it gets pure so no fear left all the fear comes from inside and when no fear left so there no problem left.

Because there is no value of exterior things for a (Sannyasi) recluse, (sannyasin) renunciation is very strong genre, no fear can touch to (sannyasi) recluse, (Sannyasi) recluse make great balance in life, this is why he keeps involve in all the mundane things but does not attach with mundane things, which belong to this rotten society.

To accept spirituality and become (sannaysi) recluse is not that hard that man is running away from this.

This is the reason, that man is living this sick life, he is suffering, he is in pain, but he still wants to live with his sick life, his fear keeps him away from (Sannyasin) renunciation.

Man had covered everything that can make man curious for (Sannyasin) renunciation, man has become man's enemy, only one acceptance can make man free from all his pain and misery, all enlightened ones try to awaken man, but our society's design made like this that it has become very difficult to accept (Sannyasin) renunciation, people run away from (Sannyasin) renunciation.

All your so-called religious teachers make you confuse with their stories of God, they told you, if you want to meet God you have to renounce all the mundane things and dedicate your life to God and prays to him the only way that you can be free from death and birth, our society made everything very complicated it is hard to find the right direction for you, all religion teachers are confused, they kept you confused and this confusion does not allow you to accept (Sannyasin) renunciation.

These religion teachers have a big fear of sage and (Sannyasi) recluse, these teachers feel difficulty to face the (sannyasi) recluse because a sage a (sannyasi) recluse does not care about society, because (sannyasi) recluse does not have anything to lose,

They cannot persuade a (sannyasi) recluse telling him that you will go to heaven, they cannot even scare him with Hell, yes, but they always condemnation them telling, they will go to hell, but all these try cannot help these religious teachers, because they cannot give fear to whom, who doesn't have anything to lose and who does not care about Heaven and Hell.

(Sannyasi) Recluse has already found the truth, which man was looking on the wrong path, and (sannyasi) recluse spreading the truth and there are few daring people who ready to accept, ready to catch on the truth, but the people who still living in fear pulling them back, do not allow them to accept (sannyasin) renunciation, they try to bond them with mundane things,

Once someone tastes of (sannyasin) renunciation, it is very difficult to go back, because Inner life is very beautiful, one just totally lost in the beauty of it, which never ends, but there are some people those misunderstood to (Sannyasin) renunciation, they pretend to be (sannyasi) the recluse.

There is incident about this.

King of the king.

One day I was in my singing class, that day I was late, so when I was practicing with my teacher, one old man knocked the door and my teacher's servant gave him food and the old man went, my teacher told me that he comes almost every day, the teacher told me that his name is Shahanshah and he is a saint, Shahnshah! The king of the King, I was a little curious about him, why he has named Shahnshah? Is this his real name? I asked to my teacher that is this his real name? The teacher replied yes, it is his real name, then my teacher told me the whole story, one day my teacher asked the same question to Shahnshah, is this your real name? He replied yes. He told my teacher that I have given this name to myself because I live my life like Shahnshah, he said that I don't care about anything, whatever I find to wear, I wear, whatever I get to eat, I eat, and wherever place I find to sleep, I sleep, there is no demand left in my life, I do not demand, I do not ask anything special, just accept whatever I get, I don't have any wish, I have dedicated my whole life to God.

He said that there is no attraction left in him for any mundane things; I just rumination to God, nothing else.

My teacher asked him, by all that, it seems that you are a saint, not a shahnsha, so he replied, everything belong to God, everything is creation of God and I'm totally attached to him, I'm his man, so everything is mine, that's how I am a Shahnsha,

I was thinking, it is great that he does not care about society because there is nothing to care about, because real treasure is in you, it is inside you, everything is Maya Illusion, he does not run behind mundane things. Great! But

He was saying that there is no attraction left in him, if there is no attraction left, so why he feels that he is shahnsha, whom he wants to show and tell that he is not like others, he is special, because he is a saint, so he is shahnsha, his attraction still there it just transforms. He is living in misunderstanding. It affected him, that's why he was worried about others, what people think about him, and he told the story so there must be something in his mind that he tries to convince people.

The fear is very strong whatever you become this will not leave you alone, only the real (sannyasi) recluse get totally liberate from this fear. Otherwise, it keeps you in its grip in different-different faces.

Before schooling study, before campus study, before professional study every child need to study sannyasin, sannyasin, renunciation should be priority in our society,

If (sannyasin) renunciation would be available for every child, for every woman and man, if (sannyasi) recluse teacher would be available to teach this education so man cannot imagine of his success that he could achieve.

Teaching of (Sannyasin) renunciation should be available in every school, if this would happen so this whole world totally changes into a heavenly place,

As I told before sannyasin is an event this is not something that can give and take. Yes, but the teaching of (Sannyasin) can teach.

Example. If, there would be no girl live in the world without knowing the girl's existence, how can any man fall in love with a girl.

In this way teaching of sannyasin should available, so after knowing, after understand to sannyasin this can happen with man. Sannyasin can happen with man.

Man has to give priority to sannyasin to make a better place of this world, this is for human, this for this earth, this education has a great potential, but the man is running away from sannyasin, for sannyasin one no need to change in his life, whatever he is doing can do, there is no need at all to change things, things will change itself.

Revelation of Fashion

The meaning of fashion for man has become something else, man always wants to become somebody else, man is always keep running away from the truth, man does not want to accept to himself, man's escaping from self is creating problems in his life, it started the problems, it has become a reason of man's madness.

Fashion has made man ugly, definition of fashion is nonconformist and conformist, people who try to be different from others, called themselves fashionable wearing cloth in different style, whether it is good or not, they do not want to be look alike others, their only motive to be different, they can do anything for being different, they can do any experiment with their hair, with their body, with their clothes, they can do anything, and for being different they become worse and the other word is conformist the same people stay in fashion group, only with those strange fashionable people, their only motive competition with each other, they just stretch themselves both side conformist and nonconformity with no reason, fashion has no meaning, today's meaning of fashion has become different and this has become man's sickness.

People smoke name of fashion takes drugs name of fashion, they can do anything and everything for fashion to become a part of those sick people, become part of the sick society, who called themselves fashionable,

I heard people, they give advice to others while they were smoking, this is very bad habit one should never smoke, they always give advice when they were smoking, when someone asks them why you started smoking, they answered my friend made me started smoking, this is the old story, but the real story is.

If you ask now so people say that they have started smoke because when they were with other people those are smoker, I feel like left behind so I also start smoke, smoking is today's fashion, smoking is fashion people who smoke are fashionable and those who do not smoke with them they are old fashioned people, that's why they started smoking and to be with those sick smoker, other started smoking because when they do smoke with them they become a part of their group their society and people take them as fashionable people, it is today's fashion, and they speak with proud, it is today's fashion, and I have seen people smoking cigarette and few other drugs saying this is today's fashion. I do not have any problem with smoking, it is individual's choice, my point is, do not start things because other do, I just wanted to reveal state of man's mind that is it.

And the funny thing is that those people they called themselves fashionable, these same people, they do smoke and take other drugs, these same people most of them, they also do yoga, isn't it strange?

When you talk about yoga with these so-called fashionable people, they take special interest, about yoga and meditations, I'm not saying doing yoga and meditation is not good, Yoga and Meditation are very good for body and spirit.

But the problem is that when these so-called fashionable people do yoga and meditation, they don't do because of good health, few do, for this reason, but most of them do because it is today's fashion and they feel proud to do Yoga and Meditation and talk about it, they also tell you the benefits of Yoga and Meditation, it is unacceptable, this is strange one side you are destroying your body and soul, but in other hands you are talking about yoga and meditation, but the thing is that they do not do Yoga and Meditation, they just want to part of society, part of the latest trend, people just blindly follow latest trend, without knowing about it.

Those are fashionable and live with the latest trends. Whatever the latest trends are they just stick with that, in the desire of doing something different, something new they are doing something else, which they cannot describe, to make self-up to date, they can go so far, it seems, there is no limits of going far.

Because of the latest trend and in the desire of doing different things, this society has become mad.

He who is spiritual more over being religious it is great, it means they do not follow religion in formulistic ways and traditional ways, they are spiritual over religious, they discover their own path to know the God,

But he who takes spirituality as fashion, are cheating himself, the human mind has great potential for manipulating things, it always finds a way of escaping, it diverts things according to its convenience.

Everything has become a fashion in present time, even spirituality.

And it is dangerous for those who called themselves fashionable.

This fashion made things more difficult, in present time people know everything about spirituality, there are lots of books and text available for everyone, if you search in the internet you will find lots of material about spirituality, and people have read and heard about it, and now they know it, but there is one problem they know all this but they knowing is superficial, anything superficially is totally waste and this superficial thing become wall, and people has shut down their mind, spirituality is not a thing to read or heard only it is thing of experience, if one wants to know this, so he has to take effort and experience it, feel it, take it down till its center of his core.

This is very strange, people do whatever others do, some are shy they cannot take their own decision, they only copy to others because they do not have dared to do their own things, they are kind of shy people, because they do not find themselves that they fit in this sick society, that is why they try to fit themselves in this confuse and sick society.

If they do not do the same thing, they will not be accepting in society. They are doing things because they want to show to others; because others are doing, that's why they are doing.

Actually the great chaos has spread in this world, everybody is following to each other, from where all these started, no one knows, people do not have time to find out this, they are just follow new trend.

Yoga is as old as Indian culture, Yoga and Meditation are today's trend but fifteen years back if you talk about, Yoga and if you say I do Yoga, so people used to think that you are some old fashioned and low-class kind of person, but if you talk about Yoga nowadays people take extra interest in the topic of Yoga and Meditation.

> Ch-7, sh-6- Be aware that everything
> living is manifested by these two energies
> of mine; I am the creator, the sustainer
> and the destroyer of all the worlds.

7- O Arjuna there is nothing superior
to me; everything existing is connected
to me like pearls on a thread.

10- O Arjuna, try to understand me as the
eternal origin of all living entities. I am
the wisdom of the spiritually intelligent
and the prowess of the powerful.

Conclusion – God is generating cause of whole existence, God is in you, God in me, God in everything, in every particle, you and me are not apart from God, nothing is apart, is just man does not know this secret properly, those who knows this, he who knows this, just knows superficially, the great truth is hiding inside man, man just has to understand, and he is not much far from this truth, despite of involving in all mundane things God is free from everything, this is nature of God, we also have this potential to get free, despite of involving in all the mundane things man could be free from everything because man believes that he is doer this why he is attached with all his deeds, It is up to man, what path he chooses,

Ch-9, Sh-4- All of the universes are
pervaded by me, in an imperceptibly
subtle manifestation and all living
entities find their support in me;
but I am not supported in them.

6- Understand just as the mighty wind
blowing everywhere is always situated

within space; similarly, all created
beings thus are situated in me.

11- Fools deride me in my divine
human form, unable to comprehend
my supreme nature as the ultimate
controller of all living entities.

16- I am the seven Vedic fire rituals, I
am the five daily acts of sacrifice, I am
the oblations offered to the departed
ancestors, I am the healing herb; I
am the transcendental incantation;
I am clarified cow ghee; I am the
fire and I am the act of offering.

24- I am the enjoyer and ultimate master
of all performances of sacrifice; but they
do not know me in reality, consequently
they revolve in the cycle of rebirth.

27- O Arjuna whatever action you do,
whatever you eat, whatever you offer in
sacrifice, whatever you give in charity,
whatever austerities you perform, all that
you do; make as an offering into me.

Conclusion – God is in everything, in every particle, there
is life in every particle, and fools do not recognize God,
Lord Krishna declared that he is the reason and he is all
the ritual, man does not need to do it in strange ways,
whatever is knowable, realizable is God, God is happiness,

freedom, liberation, God is seed of this existence and reason of the destruction, whosoever not able to recognize God and understand him fall and destruct, whatever you do, your all deeds calculates by God.

Chapter-10, Shlok-4,5- Spiritual intelligence, knowledge, freedom from false perception, compassion, truthfulness, control of the senses, control of the mind, happiness, unhappiness birth, death, fear and fearlessness, nonviolence, equanimity, contentment, austerity, charity, fame, infamy; all these variegated diverse qualities of all living entities originate from me alone.

20- O Arjuna, I am ultimate consciousness situated within the heart of all living entities and I am the beginning, the middle and the end as well of all living entities.

32- O Arjuna, I am alone the creator, maintainer and destroyer of all creation, of knowledge I am spiritual knowledge and of arguments I am the logical conclusion.

39- O Arjuna, and whatever is the root cause of all living entities, I am that also; there is nothing which is moving or stationary in all of creation, that exists without me

42- What necessity is there for you,
O Arjuna of such detailed knowledge
and so many examples? I support
this entire universal manifestation
situated in but a fraction of myself.

Conclusion – Lord Krishna said. I am everything man, woman, animal, water, air, etc. I'm everything whatever you know or you do not know. If everybody is God, God in everything so why man hates to each other, why man fights name of religion, the name of God. Man has to think again if the man really wants happiness and calm if the man wants to live with peace so he will choose the path of intelligence, he has to choose sannyasin, renunciation, one needs the greatest amount of dare to choose sannyasin.

Ch-11, Sh- 32- Lord Krishna said, I am
terrible time the destroyer of all beings in
all worlds, engaged to destroy all beings
in this world; of those heroic soldiers
presently situated in the opposing army,
even without you none will be spared.

33- Therefore arise for battle, O Arjuna.
You will gain fame by conquering
the enemy and enjoy a flourishing
kingdom. All these warriors have been
slain already by me due to previous
design you are merely an instrument.

Conclusion – Man's presence does not mean he is a doer, whatever is happening is because it has to happen, there nothing good and evil in this, these are just events, which happens man's life, but man is getting crazy for these events, there is no reason for pain and pleasure, there is much more pleasure than this worldly pleasure and pain, this heavenly pleasure cannot explain only one can feel it.

Ch-13, Sh-16- Within and without
all living entities, that ultimate truth
is stationary as well as mobile; on
account of it is being subatomic, that
ultimate truth is incomprehensible
and is far away yet also very near.

17- Without division that ultimate truth
appears to be divided among all the
various living entities and is to be known
as the preserver of all living entities and
the destroyer as well as the creator.

18- The ultimate truth is declared as the
illuminator of all that illuminates, beyond
the darkness of ignorance; residing within
the heart of everyone it is comprehensible
by the wisdom gained from the realization
by the knowledge of direct experience.

19- My devotee understanding this field
of activity, knowledge and what is to
be known thus described in summary
becomes qualified for my divine nature.

29- By seeing the ultimate consciousness
equally everywhere, impartially
situated, one does not degrade the
embodied self, by the self; therefore,
reaching the supreme goal.

31 - When one actually perceives the expansion and
diversity of all life forms as situated in the unity of
material nature; therefore, at that time the ultimate truth
is attained.

Conclusion – Man divides everything whatever possibly he can divide, man also divides God, but god is undivided only ignorant, foolish people think they can divide God, but they cannot,

God is away from all the hate, all the anger, and all the greed, God does not really require all this, God is the equipoise, the balance, God is intelligence, God is utter happiness,

Whosoever knows that God in every creature in everything is the (Sannyasi) recluse.

Chapter-14, Shlok-3- O Arjuna, the
entire expansive material energy is
the womb into which I infuse the
embryo of individual consciousness;
subsequently manifested by me,
every species of life generated.

8- You should know, O Arjuna, that
the mode of ignorance as the cause
of delusion enslaving all embodied

beings born of nescience; by negligence,
listlessness and somnolence.

Conclusion – The whole existence is made by material and intelligence, body and soul, and man has to accept both body and soul, both make great balance, in the absence of one another become imbalance. Today's world's God is materialistic; intelligence has disappeared, in the absence of intelligence all mankind is suffering.

Ch-15, Sh-7- Verily the embodied
living entity is my infinitesimal
potency and eternal; in the world of
embodied living entities the influence
of the material energy is carried by the
mind and the six perceptual senses.

Conclusion – In this whole existence, everything and everyone is part of God,

In this material world, every man is struggling, fighting with all his senses,

There is nothing deprive of God in this whole existence.

The state of the man

Chapter-2, Shlok14

matra-sparsas tu kaunteya sitosna-sukha-duhkha-dah

Agamapayino 'nityas tams titiksasva bharata

O Arjuna, only the interaction of
the senses and sense objects give
cold, heat, pleasure and pain.

These things are temporary,
appearing and disappearing;
therefore, try to tolerate them.

Shlok-15

yam hi na vyathayanty ete
purusam purusarsabha

sama-duhkha-sukham dhiram
so mrtatvaya kalpate

O noblest of men, that person
of wise judgment equipoised
in happiness and distress,

Who cannot be disturbed by these
is certainly eligible for liberation.

Human nature is like the weather, sometimes winter,
sometimes summer and sometime rainy, it always changes
with time, man's all senses controls his nature, man does not

have any control on his senses, man does not need to flow with it, man must understand it intelligently.

If the man would forcefully try to tolerate his senses, so it would very harmful for him, this toleration will become poison for him and for others, by this he will only torture himself, so man needs to understand his senses, and intelligently live with it, it says that controlling our senses is not easy for normal man, this is very hard only great saint can control this, but this is not right, this not true at all, man has to learn, man has to understand from his childhood so it would not be this much difficult for him, so this is not right to say that this is just for (sannyasi) recluse, this is for each and every one,

If man learns to control his senses, so he can live his life with great pleasure, pain and misery will come in his life but he will know how to live with it, and who he intelligently understands his senses will celebrate each and everything in his life, every moment will be celebration for him.

O noblest of men, that person of wise judgment equipoise in happiness and distress, who cannot be disturbed by these, is certainly eligible for liberation.

This shlok says, who wisely take judgment in distress and happiness and do not disturb is certainly eligible for liberation,

Liberation from pain, misery and distress, when a man equipoise in all situations so he goes free, he goes liberate,

This does not mean that this is just for (Sannyasi) recluse, this for every human being, in Geeta this knowledge has provided thousands of years ago, but man totally has ignored it, because man completely ignored it that is why man is living his life in misery and pain, this knowledge can totally remove misery from man's life,

When I say, man, so I mean, man and woman both, so I use man word for writing connivance.

Man has to take decision that he wants to live in this old and rotten society with its old and rotten rules or he would welcome new thinking, new ideas, in ancient time in India man had lived with this intelligent thought, in our ancient time man was really intelligent, but in today's world man is living with unintelligent, this is why he did too much destruction, and with this behavior he will destroy the whole world, man has to accept (sannyasin) renunciation.

With (sannyasin) renunciation all intelligent will come, man improves his life.

This body is mortal

Chapter-2, Shlok-22

vasamsi jirnani yatha vihaya navani grhnati naro 'parani

tatha sarirani vihaya jirnany anyani samyati navani dehi

> Just as a man giving up old worn out
> garments accepts other new apparel,

> In the same way, the embodied
> soul, giving up old and worn out
> bodies verily accepts new bodies.

Geeta's all sutras can change a man's life, just he needs to understand Geeta's sutras properly and inclusion these sutras in his soul, and he has to use these sutras in his day today's life, Geeta's sutra is a great treasure of intelligence, the great treasure of true knowledge,

Geeta's sutras can become great pillars in human life, these sutras can remove misery from man's life, and man's life can become more and more beautiful, man's life can fill with fragrance,

man has wasted his whole life just to collected lots of and lots of money and power, man has become mad for money, and his madness become reason of his misery, this money is the main reason of man's all problems, I do not mean to renounce money, just need to understand how much is your requirement for money, I don't have any problem with money, but man's madness is the problem, man has totally corrupted, and money's carton has fallen on his eyes and he cannot see through this carton, his eyes has totally closed, he cannot see anything other than money, man believes that this money can give him everything, but money cannot give man happiness, money can give man just mundane things, just worldly things.

This is true that man can have the mundane things with money, but only mundane things, not happiness, money are man's requirement, man cannot survive without money in this world, because the structure of this society is made up of such, that is why he needs money for surviving, but man's greed becomes massive problems for man, for this society, for this earth.

And now limitless wealth, limitless power become man's weakness, man has become mad for money, mad for power, this is the reason for this world's misery, this world's destruction, without right knowledge, without intelligence power become very dangerous for our society, peep into man's history everything will reveal, hunger of power and wealth did massive destruction, and this destruction is still happening, if man will remember Geeta's sutras that his body is mortal and one day this body will die and nothing will be left, except his intelligence, man's all treasure, his whole wealth, his whole power is the big lie, his treasure is false,

If man would read and learn Geeta's sutras and understand and inclusion these sutras bottom of his core, so the view of man's life will completely change, his whole life will change, and this whole world, this whole society will change.

So man has to read, learn and understand these sutras, he will know that collecting wealth unnecessarily for happiness for himself and his family is useless, what does he need for happiness is intelligence, intelligence make this world very beautiful, Geeta is the treasure of intelligence.

Man's wisdom can give him utterly happiness and utterly calm, man's approach is on the wrong path, man is approaching money and power that is why our society's structure built in such way, if man's approach will change, so he can achieve utterly happiness, utterly joy, his approach should be toward (Sannyasin) renunciation side, with (sannyasin) renunciation wisdom comes, man does not need to worship Geeta, what man need is little meditation and focused on the right path and the Geeta tells all, just he has to understand its sutras properly, to cram Geeta's sutra or worship Geeta is not the right way, until man does not understand Geeta's sutras, Geeta cannot help him at all, it would be just a book for him, Geeta is here since longer than 5000 years, but it could not change to our society yet, because Geeta has become the holy book, become worship book, I agree this is the holy book, Geeta is worship-able, why because it has great knowledge in it, but the man has to study it deeply, then this book can change his life, otherwise as we are chanting and rat all other Granth and mantras, but these did not help yet,

Our society is still suffering, people are suffering, the world totally has lost its balance, this balance can come back, but the man has to change himself, otherwise this society will be imbalance, and man will be keep suffering.

Geeta has hidden secrets, just you need to understand, and these secrets can make this world so beautiful and happy. As I have told you in other chapters, man has to learn what is truth and what is lie, man has to make distance from illusory and go near to truth, man has to awaken from his sleep, it does not matter, what man does, he just need to understand, he just need to keep in his mind what is illusory and what is truth.

"Because" there is more than enough is also not good. More love, more wealth, more lie, more power anything more than enough creates problem if man remembers that this body is mortal and all collections of his wealth is wasted,

And he does not need to keep lots of money, only saving some money and property, which would be enough for surviving of his family,

because there is more than enough wealth, makes the man worry about its security, too much wealth is the reason of discrimination, for this money man need banks, security, lockers all these things to keep this wealth safe and secure, to keep safe to this wealth man creates borders, military and navy, man invented dangerous weapon, and these dangerous weapons become threat for the world, I'm not saying remove all militaries, all forces and all borders, I am even not saying donate your whole wealth,

Practically this is not possible, and not every man has this much dare to take this decision, very few people will have this much dare to donate their wealth, you can count them in your finger, but the thing is by donating wealth, these societies problems will not solve, problems will stand still, the problems will solve with intelligence, every new decision, every new idea takes time to digest by commune, once this society understands what is right for them, then they will accept new idea.

This is the time when this world needs to accept Geeta's knowledge, its sutras, and intelligence. Geeta's sutra can bring the great changes in this society, one is poor and one is rich, this difference, this discrimination force man to become criminal, this is the reason of man's misery, this is not right that very few people have all the money, all the wealth and other than these few people are not rich, rest are not rich like them, and this richness, these mundane things and attractions these expensive products attracts man, and this attraction is the reason of all the problems, and for all these things man wants money, and man cheats man, man kills man. All the play, all the circus is happening for these mundane things, and these mundane things never end but man's life ends running behind these things, and when these mundane, these earthly things get out of man's reach, so the attraction of these things moves a man to do wrong deeds.

Man actually does not need to cheat man for money, he does not need to kill man for money, he does not need to build dangerous weapon if man would not make of money's stack, so he will not have to worry about it, the stack of money makes man worry, stack of money creates problems, this collection of money, this collection of power is problem of this world,

If every man and woman keep in their mind that this over stack of money and power is the reason of their misery, in this world where we live, man does not want to help to others, man does not value man, man hates man, man has become man's enemy, man cheats man, man kills, man for the money and for the power, where we will reach with this attitude with this manner of life, this world need to change its attitude manner of life,

This body is mortal.

As is written in the Geeta that man never dies only body changes, these sutras given in Geeta can change a human's life, the man should always remember that this body is mortal.

Ch-2, Sh12-na tv evaham jatu
nasam na tvam neme janadhipah
na caiva na bhavisyamah sarve vayam atah param
Certainly never at any time did I not exist, nor you, nor all these kings and certainly never shall we cease to exist in the future.

This sutra tells that this not only life, this existence is a journey, this not only earth, there are countless earth, it all depends where man goes after this life, above life or below, how you live this life, it all depends, there are better and better earth then this earth, and there is worse earth too.

Ch-2, Sh-13- Just as in the physical body
of the embodied being is the process of
childhood, youth and old age, similarly
by the transmigration from one body
to another the wise are never deluded.

Again, this sutra is not different from others, this sutra is pointing toward the same thing, this body is mortal, man grows and get old and one day he dies, and his soul transforms into another life, this is not the only life,

There is no evidence of the soul, because the soul is not made with the material, soul is an intelligence, whom nobody can see or touch, and intelligence never dies, it chooses its home, and its home is the human body, and it lives there, after man dies, his intelligence never dies or destroy, it is immortal. It travels one to another life.

Ch-2, Sh-16- In the unreal there is
no duration and in the real there is
no cessation; indeed, the conclusion
between both the two has been
analyzed by knower of the truth.

25- It is declared that the soul is
imperceptible; the soul is inconceivable,
the soul is immutable; therefore,
understanding the soul as such, it
is improper for you to lament.

Conclusion – In the Shlok of Geeta, Lord Krishna said, man does not have to mourn for death because the soul is immortal so there is no reason for sorrow;

The man's body changes in every moment since his birth to old age, the body never stays the same, only memory and soul stay in the body, if one sees with this point of view so his pain will less, he could be able to control his sorrow, his pain his life can totally change.

Intelligence and soul never die so there is no reason to feel bad for anything.

Ch-4, Sh-5- Lord Krishna said; many
births of mine and also of yours have
passed O Arjuna; I have knowledgeable
of all of them; but you do not know.

6- Although being birth less, imperishable
and immutable, the lord of all living
entities; being so situated I appear in
this world in my original transcendental
form by my internal potency.

Conclusion – This is not only life, there is life after live, soul transform from one to another and man's intelligence transform one to another.

Ch-6, Sh-41- After achieving the planets
of those who performed pious activities;
one who has fallen from the science of
uniting the individual consciousness with
the ultimate consciousness, after residing
there for many, many years takes birth
in a family of the pious and prosperous.

42- Otherwise one surely takes birth
in a family endowed with wisdom in
the science of uniting the individual
consciousness with the ultimate
consciousness; certainly such a birth
as this is very rare in this world.

43- O Arjuna, in this way the revival of
spiritual intelligence is regained that was
practiced in a previous life; thereafter he
endeavors once again for perfection.

44- Because of the strength of the
previous practice one is irresistibly

attracted; certainly even the inquisitive
in the science of uniting the individual
consciousness with the ultimate
consciousness surpasses the ritualistic
principles for certain actions in the Vedas.

45- One perfected in the science of
uniting the individual consciousness with
the ultimate consciousness diligently
endeavoring by rigid practice, purified
of worldly attachment; achieves the
perfection of many, many lifetimes
and attains the supreme goal.

Conclusion – (Sannysin) Recluse takes birth in a rich family, the failure (Sannyasi) recluse, he who does not able achieve a higher state of (sannyasin) renunciation, he who takes birth in rich and intelligent atmosphere and get back his all abilities, but this event is very rare, that great sannysin, recluse can take birth in this world and achieving a higher state of sannysin, renunciation it takes many births.

Ch-8, Sh-6- O Arjuna, one who
at the final moment gives up
their body remembering any idea
whatsoever certainly becomes the
object of that idea, being absorbed
in it by constant contemplation.

Conclusion – Lord Shri Krishna said in Geeta that whatever emotions, feelings man keeps, he achieves to that state, and at the end, whatever feelings come, all those thoughts made by his whole life's action, his whole life's action's reaction result gets at the end of man's life.

Whatever thought human keeps according to that he goes to that state.

> Ch-9, Sh-21- Having enjoyed extensively the heave nly spheres, the results of their pious activities being exhausted, return to the worlds of mortals; thus following the doctrine of righteousness in the three Vedas, desirers of sense enjoyment receives only the cycle of birth and death.

> 25- Worshippers of the demigods go the demigods, worshipers of the ancestors go to the ancestors, worships of the ghosts and spirits go to the ghost and spirits and my worshipers certainly come to me.

Conclusion – To whom the man does worship, he achieves to same, whose worship man can do? As he himself has, so whatever man does he achieve to same.

> Ch-13, Sh-22- The individual consciousness situated in the material energy certainly experiences the three modes of material nature produced by the material energy; the beguiling infatuation of these three modes of material nature is the cause of a being innumerable births, superior and inferior in the wombs of variegated life forms.

23- Within the body, supreme to
the individual consciousness; an
indwelling observer; a sanctioner,
a preserver, an enjoyer and indeed
ultimate controller as well is described
as the ultimate consciousness.

24- Anyone who understands in this
way the individual consciousness and the
ultimate consciousness also the material
energy along with the three modes of
material nature, one although existing in
any condition never takes birth again.

Conclusion – There is some power in the man, who has
the whole charge in his hands that power give the orders,
the man does not have control on his decisions, whosoever
understand this deeply, do not take birth here in this world
again.

Ch-14, Sh-9- O Arjuna, the mode of
goodness ensnares one in happiness, the
mode of passion in certain activity and
the mode of ignorance in negligence
and the like, obscuring knowledge.

Conclusion – The material nature is the cause of all the
events, (what happens in man's life, and after knowing
this, if one able to cross his nature), so he achieves utterly
happiness.

Ch-15, Sh-8- Whatever body the eternal
infinitesimal potency enters and from
whatever body he departs; carrying this
subtle body from the old body as the air,
fragrance; transfers it to a new body.

10- The foolish mesmerized by the three
modes of material nature cannot perceive
this infinitesimal potency departing the
body, residing in the body or enjoying
in the body; but those enlightened
by the eye of wisdom can perceive.

Conclusion – Spirit and wisdom transform in body,

Fools never understand that how can intelligence and soul change body, one need a deep intelligence, sense to understand this, and the people in this world are too busy,

They also never understand that human body's every action has bonded with the material nature.

Ch-16, Sh-10- Addicted to insatiable
lusts, the demoniac, irrational
due to arrogance, vanity and
conceit, out of illusion endeavor for
impermanent things engaging in
impure acts by premeditated vows.

11, 12- Overwhelmed with a life
full of unlimited fears and anxieties;
the demoniac considers that the
gratification of the senses as the
highest goal of life; being bound by the

entanglement of hundreds of schemes,
overcome by lust and anger striving
to accumulate wealth illicitly for the
purpose of gratifying their senses.

24- Therefore the injunctions of the
Vedic scriptures in ascertaining what
should be done and what should not be
done are your authority; knowing the
ordinances of the Vedic scriptures as
prescribed, you should perform actions
in this world as a matter of duty.

Conclusion – There is no possible way that you satisfy with desire and lust, those who are living to satisfy their senses and their body, they are totally wasting their life,

Foolish people contemplate about money, relations, enemies, and power and all the mundane things, but they never think about the truth which is really considerable, if one knows the truth, so all the treasure of happiness come itself to him,

These kinds of people stuck and suffer in (Maya) illusion for a very long time. An egocentric person does not get the result of his doings, this kind of person becomes the target of jealousy, because of that they would not get happiness, pleasure in this or any other life.

The ancient scriptures are treasures of wisdom, one who studies them get the heights in the life,

There are few paths of suffering in the world anger, greed, lust and imbalance of everything, balance is the key to happiness.

Ch-17, Sh-15- Truthful speech which
is inoffensive to others, pleasing
and beneficial as well as regular
recitation of the Vedic scriptures
is declared austerity of speech.

23- Om Tat Sat, the eternal,
transcendental sound vibration
of the ultimate consciousness, the
threefold representation known to
indicate the ultimate truth; in ancient
times the Brahmans, the Vedic
scriptures and the performance of
sacrifice were ordained by them.

Conclusion – Using the language in a proper way is
austerity of words, language, practice of these shloks bless
great knowledge.

Ch-18, 12- Results of the three kinds of
activates accrue after death, leading to
hellish planets, leading to heavenly spheres
and to the human world in between for
those desiring the results of action; but
never t anytime for the renunciate.

Conclusion – Fool has to suffer for his deeds in this and
next life, but (Sannysi) recluse never bond with his deeds.

Devotee and Lover

Chapter-9, Shlok-34

man-mana bhava mad-bhakto mad-yaji mam namaskuru

mam evaisyasi yuktvaivam atmamam mat-parayanah

> Be ever conscious of me, be my devotee,
> worship me, offer obeisance unto me;
>
> In this way completely dedicating mind
> and body unto me, having me for the
> supreme goal you will certainly reach me.

Devotion meaning is love and love meaning devotion,

Love is the most beautiful thing, love is awakening love is consciousness, not everybody can do pure love, everyone has love inside them, love is all around us less or more, it is everywhere in everyone, but not everyone can love from his deep down soul, love has been corrupted, love has been faked, very few people have potential to do deep love, true love, I'm not talking about love to God, love of man or woman, child mother father, sister, friend. Love is just love it can happen with anyone anywhere, when a lover fall in love with a beautiful girl, there is no different between a lover and a sage both are equal, lover is just devotee and devotee is lover both are same there is no discrimination between both of them, when a man or a woman fall in love so whatever happens inside them, that is very first step of awakening toward and this last step of awakening, the real lovers are above then all, in the same way, the real devotee is above then all, the devotion is the state where nothing left everything good and evil flow away, all the garbage all the useless things, in fact, all the things gone away. The soul of devotee, lover gets totally pure,

Love is awakening, love is pure, love is beautiful, love is happiness, love is joy, love is consciousness, and love is fragrance, love is blooming of the flowers' interiority of the lover and the devotee.

In the love, the lover becomes very delicate than anything else, nothing is more delicate than a lover, everything becomes beautiful, the lover totally surrendered himself in love, no demand left no condition left in love.

Lover and devotee both are the rebel, they really do not care about the rule of society, and their consciousness toward unconscious society slowly-slowly disappear, and become consciousness toward conscious, awakening.

For the devotee and lover, there is no requirement left to go to the temple, church, mosque. Because they direct connect to his lover, love is an event of extrovert life; it is an event of introvert life.

Love is a beautiful word. But not everyone can understand of this beautiful word and state. Although everybody has a potential for love, but they do not have purity in their love, and their love depends on external beauty and things, and their love keeps changing one to another. There are no problems loving more than one person, but remember love is not an extrovert event, it is an introvert event. Love is spontaneous, love brings revolution in your life, love brings beauty in your life, but if love brings slavery in your life so that's not love that's must be something else, imposing self on others is not love, that is sickness of man, this is a man-made way of imposing love to each other, Marriage, this is the invention of man, this is the way of imposing to someone on self.

Man and woman daggle to each other their whole life, they daggle and imposing because both have the greed with each other, whether it is their sexual need, money, or they get habitual to each other, this bond of marriage become their prison, and man cannot run away from this prison and cannot live with this, but love and lover so completely far away from this prison, from this slavery, lover and devotee are in total freedom, liberation. But when I say, love I do not talk about ordinary love I talk about pure and true love.

Nowadays people use love word for everything, so it creates more confusion about love as they use this for shoes clothes, food, they use it for anything if they like anything little more than liking, and they say I love this and that, if someone uses this sentence, I love this, I love that, I love your dance, I love your singing, I love this film, I love this actors' style, this kind of people love almost everything.

When they propose to one whom they want to become their girlfriend or boyfriend, they really don't know they are in love or not, because they love almost everything, and if they are saying I love you so what does it mean? Are they really loving or they said, because they have a habit to say this?

So when you hear I love you from this kind of people so just beware of them, because they don't know. What is love, if you think they love you, so they will treat you like the way they treat all other things they love.

When they bought a pair of shoe they said I want these shoes, I love them, when they bought, they surely wear on their feet, because the shoes made to wear on feet, and you know when one wear shoes in his feet so he walks on the road, street, and everywhere he goes, so how can one keep his love on his feet and give it place in the garbage, and but after take-off his shoes he throws them with other shoes, and he forgot all his love for his shoes.

How can anybody love to shoes, if one love to his shoes so he or she should put his/her shoes on the top and should do worship them, give their love to their shoes, but this is not possible so this kind of people do not even know, what is the meaning of love. So be very careful with this kind of people,

People are faking around, and this fake personality has become part of their life, and this fakeness is also a very big problem of their all pain and suffering, when someone says, I love this shoe or I love some particular thing or somebody's particular quality, it means they are faking,

Who keeps love on his mouth all the time; they have a big part in the society to creating confusion, in their mind and in their life, and this confusion does not leave them until, their whole life becomes completely fake,

Language left no meaning if a man will use it wrongly, language expresses man's opinions and his feelings, language meanings lot, but man has corrupted language too, this the way by which one can express and share his knowledge, if whatever he will say, it left a big impact on others, it all depends how others believe on him, and in your regular life its impact to your all relationships, it impacts to your kids, your friend, your life partner, your parents, it can impact on everything and on everybody. So language has great value man should not lose its value.

The only meaning of Devotion is love, the devotee is a lover, there is nothing left between the devotee and lover except love, love is, whether one love to a woman, a man, mother, father, sister, brother or friend. Love is love and it is the same love, if the love is true so it will take you toward ultimate when one is in love so there is nothing left for him except his love, love and lover become one and everything disappears.

Every man has a different mind, some people like easy and some like difficult, not every man can become a devotee and not every man can become enlightened, this is why there are two paths has given to man, it is up to man what he chooses, according to his nature man will choose his path, both paths will take a man to the ultimate. But this not only reason that different path has made to achieve enlighten,

Because the man is egocentric, if shri Krishna said that man does not need any medium to worship, the man himself can achieve ultimate, so these words make the man more egocentric, very few people who really can understand will achieve ultimate and all others can never achieve ultimate.

For man's absoluteness, shri Krishna has given the man very easy way to achieve ultimate, man can achieve ultimate without any medium, but this is not easy for everybody because each man is different from his nature,

There are hidden secrets in these shloks, when Shri Krishna says worship me, when he talks about himself so he also means all of you, because this creation, all the human race, all the mundane things, everything whatever you know are not different from creator, there is no difference at all between man and creator, so when he talks about himself so his also means man, man's inner core, man's soul, so if man worships its soul, so he can achieve ultimate, when I say worship, it does not mean only pray to any God, I mean meditation, I mean stay focus inside yourself. Do not to indulge in any act by deeds.

Shri Krishna told man both ways, path of wisdom and path of devotion, both ways take man to liberation and ultimate.

If you choose to devote, so does it like Mira Bai (great devotee of Lord Krishna from our ancient time). Mira was great, there is no middle path to ultimate Happiness and there is no middle path of intelligence; man has to choose either path of devotion or the path of wisdom, both ways are right. Devotee gets completely pure by his love, there is nothing left to devotee and love one.

> Ch-2, Sh-50- One endowed with spiritual
> intelligence can get rid of both positive
> and negative reaction in this very life;
> therefore, be diligent in the science of
> uniting the individual consciousness
> with the ultimate consciousness; in
> all activities the science of uniting the
> individual consciousness with the ultimate
> consciousness is superlative genius.

> 66- One with an uncontrolled mind
> cannot have spiritual intelligence, one
> devoid of spiritual intelligence never

meditates on the ultimate truth and for
one who never meditates on the ultimate
truth there is no peace and for one
destitute of peace where is happiness?

Conclusion – By devotion man gets pure and freed from
all doings and sins, when all the pride, arrogance falls than
a pure man born.

Ch-4, Sh-41- O Arjuna, activities cannot
bind one who has renounced the fruits of
activities; overcoming all doubts by the
transcendental knowledge of the science
of uniting one's individual consciousness
with the ultimate consciousness
attains the state of self-realization.

Conclusion – In this world or any other world, nothing
is greater than wisdom, intelligence. The devotee does not
need any intelligence because devotion is above than all
intelligence; devotee has real happiness, the happiness is
above than this world's happiness and pain; the real devotee
is like God.

Whosoever knows God's nature, that one become
like him;

Ch-5, Sh-6- But renunciation of action,
O mighty armed one, afflicts one with
distress without prescribed action in
the science of uniting the individual
consciousness with the ultimate
consciousness, one performing in

prescribed actions in the science of uniting
the individual consciousness with the
ultimate consciousness is a wise man and
without delay attains the ultimate truth.

Conclusion – Try to understand renounces, in this endeavor great secrets will reveal.

He who dedicates his all deeds and fruits of doings to God, he goes totally free, he who concerns about the fruit of his doings suffers,

When human mind, faith and everything, consider to God, this consideration gets pure and liberate human from every sin reaction.

Ch-6, Sh-29- One perfectly realized
and perfected in the science of uniting
the individual consciousness with the
ultimate consciousness, identifying
with this consciousness everywhere and
in everything perceives the realized
self-situated in all living entities and
all living entities in the realized self.

30- For one who sees me everywhere
and sees everything in me, I am
never forgotten by them and they
are never forgotten by me.

Conclusion – who sees God in everything and everybody is the real devotee, and for this kind of person God has never disappeared.

Ch-7, Sh-15- The depraved, the foolish,
the lower levels of humanity, do not
surrender unto me, their discrimination
degraded by the illusory energy they
betake to the nature of the demoniac.

20- Those deprived of discrimination by
various desires impelled by their particular
natures worship the lesser demigods
adapting to the applicable rites and rituals.

25- I am not manifest to everyone,
being veiled by my illusory potency
in the external energy. The ignorant
in this world cannot understand me,
the unborn and imperishable.

Conclusion – Foolish people cannot understand God,
Unintelligent people made different-different ways to
worship God, the foolish think they would manipulate God
with their foolish idea.

Ch-8, Sh-14- O Arjuna, for such a
one perfecting the science of uniting
the individual consciousness with
the ultimate consciousness, without
deviation, always engaged in constantly
remembering me continuously; to
him I am very easily attainable.

27- O Arjuna, coming to know about
these two paths, anyone perfecting

the science of uniting the individual
consciousness with the ultimate
consciousness is never deluded; therefore,
O Arjuna always be engaged in the science
of uniting the individual consciousness
with the ultimate consciousness.

Conclusion – Devotee always stay away from all the misery and pain, his all pleasure in devotion, devotee never disturbed by mundane things, he stays equipoise in his interior.

Ch-9, Sh-29- I am equally disposed
to all living entities; there is neither
friend nor foe to me; but those
who with loving sentiments render
devotional service unto me, such
persons are in me and I am in them.

32- O Arjuna, even those who may
be born from the wombs of degraded
women, merchants and menials; if
they take full shelter of me, they
also reach the supreme goal.

Conclusion – God is far-far away from all the discrimination; he cannot infect by this reaction. God is above than all the mundane things and attractions.

Ch-10, Sh-9- Their minds fully dedicated
unto me, their lives fully surrendered
unto me; perpetually enlightening

one another and ever relishing my
nectarine glories; completely satisfied
they enjoy transcendental bliss.

Conclusion – All the action and decisions of devotee inspire
by God, God lives in his heart that is why he fills with
utter pleasure and utter joy and he does not distract by any
reaction.

Ch-11, Sh-54- But by devotional
service O Arjuna unmixed with certain
desires and speculative knowledge, O
scorcher of enemy; it possible I can
be known and seen in such an eternal
form and factually enter my pastimes.

50- O Arjuna, one who engages in actions
for me, considering me the supreme
goal, engaging in devotional service for
me, freed from the contamination of
certain activities and mental speculation,
devoid of enmity towards any living
entity; such a person attains me.

Conclusion – Devotee become friendly, lovely, and beautiful,
because devotee does not believe in discrimination.

Ch-12, Sh-3,4- But those who worship
the indescribable, all –pervading,
inconceivable, immutable, constant,
eternal, impersonal absolute devoid
of perceptible form and attributes;

completely controlling all the senses
with spiritual intelligence equally
disposed to everything and dedicated
to the welfare of all living entities;
they certainly also achieve me.

Conclusion – The path of devotion and (Sannyasin) renunciation is the same, there is one difference between both of the path, (Sannyasi) recluse the choose the path of intelligence and the devotee choose the path of devotion.

Ch-13, Sh-25- Some by the science of
the individual consciousness attaining
communion with the ultimate
consciousness perceive within the
self, the ultimate consciousness by
meditation on the self; others by the
discrimination between matter spirit
and others by the science of uniting
the individual consciousness with the
ultimate consciousness by actions.

26- Yet others without knowing these
methods engage in worship by hearing
from others; verily they becoming
established from listening also transcend
the transmigration of death.

Conclusion – Listening to others Intelligence awaken, but fools stay unconscious.

Ch-14, Sh-19- When the embodied
being comprehends there is no other
enactor than three modes of material
nature and knows what is supreme to
the three modes of material nature;
one achieves my divine nature.

Conclusion – who he after knowing that he is not doer, so
he becomes equipoise and achieve Godliness,

Ch-15, Sh-20- O sinless one; thus
this most confidential meaning of
the scriptures had been disclosed
by me; realizing this O Arjuna; one
becomes spiritually enlightened
and accomplished in all acts.

Conclusion – Devotion or (sannyasin) renunciation chooses
one, it will light in your life, and this will spread happiness
in your life.

Ch-18, Sh-70- And for one who will
study this most righteous discourse
of ours; I shall be propitiated by
that as a performance of sacrifice of
wisdom; this is my proclamation.

71- Even the person who only
listens to this with faith and without
envy is liberated and will reach
the elevated planetary systems of
those of virtuous activities.

Conclusion – When Lord Krishan said, worship me, he does not mean, worship him in the traditional way, the way people do pray and worship, the sculpture worship is a great invention which is made to focus and balance in your interior, Lord Krishna wants to leave your all deeds on him and just dip in his love. Nothing else required.

Sinful reaction

Ch-2, Sh-41- In this yoga O Arjuna,
spiritual intelligence is firmly resolved
and exclusive; but the intellect of
those full of material desires indeed
has unlimited diverse branches.

Conclusion – Firm intelligent people do not drift on different ways, they must arrive at their destination.

Ch-5, Sh-15- The omnipresent ultimate
consciousness never accepts the
sins or either the virtues of anyone;
actual knowledge is enveloped by
ignorance and because of that the
living entities are deluded.

Conclusion – God neither embrace nor condone anybody's sin, intelligent knows the way to get rid of the sin reactions, the way is devotion and (Sannyasin) renunciation.

Ch-6, Sh-40- Lord Krishna said, O
Arjuna; they never exist destruction
for one in this life nor in the next life;
since dear friend anyone who is engaged
in virtuous acts never comes to evil.

Conclusion – Good does not defeats by evil.

Ch-18, Sh- 48- Actions prescribed
according to one's nature must not be
given up, O Arjuna, even if defective;

since all endeavors are covered with
defects as fire is covered by smoke.

Conclusion – Never renounce your own work by attracting others, your own work would always give better result than other's work,

The natural job always gives great results; the man should not renounce natural work.

Peace

Ch-4, Sh-7- Whenever and wherever
a decline of righteousness and a
predominance of unrighteousness
prevail; at that time, I manifest myself
personally, O descendant of Bharata.

8- For the protection of the devotees
and the annihilation of the miscreants
and to fully establish righteousness, I
appear millennium after millennium

Conclusion – There is always way whenever iniquity grows just man need to recognize clues of the right path.

Ch-8, Sh-27- O Arjuna, at the
commencement of universal creation
all forms of life are in delusion by the
illusions of duality born of desire and
aversion, o conqueror of enemies.

26- These light and dark paths are
begging-less and certainly as eternal
as the material universes; by one
liberation is attained and by the other
one repeatedly returns again.

Conclusion – There are two ways to leave this world, one is the way of light and one is the way of dark, the way of light is the way of intelligence and the way dark is the way of ignorant, go toward of intelligence.

Ch-9, Sh-12- These bewildered fools
of futile desires, futile endeavors, futile
knowledge and futile understanding;
certainly assume the nature of
the atheistic and demonic.

Conclusion – Those who attract to the dark side are ignorant people.

Nature

Ch-8, Sh- 20- But another unmanifest
which is eternal, of a superior nature from
the unmanifest of Brahma that is never
destroyed when all living entities perish.

Conclusion – (Parkarty) nature stays still, after the end of whole existence, nature is above of all the things in this existence.

Ch-9, Sh-10- Superintended by me
the illusory external energy manifests
all moving and non-moving entities;
for this reason, O Ajuna, the universal
manifestation is created repeatedly.

Conclusion – this whole existence is because of the God's wish, all the event and everything happening according to God's wish.

Ch-13, Sh-3- O Arjuna, certainly
knowing me as well within all bodies
as the knower of the field of activity
such knowledge of the field of
activity and the knower of the field is
actual knowledge in my opinion.

Conclusion – This is not a small event that you born, and you are reading this, there is great reason behind this, man has forgotten his potential he has to achieve it back in this life,

There is ultimate happiness, joy above than all the happiness you can get in this world by mundane things and event.

God is Omani present, he is in everything, in every creature, in every man and woman, there is no discrimination between God and this whole existence, the God is himself this existence, both are one, whatever you know or you do not know is God, never forget this.

About Author

I was born in Uttrakhand, India and when I was one-year-old my family moved to Delhi, I have studied like a regular boy, in my childhood people used to make fun of me, I was a naïve and a dumb boy, I have gone to my mother by my mind, but I look alike my father, my mother was like me in his childhood, she is very simple and feeble of mind, I am on my mother, anyways, when I was about thirteen years' old me and my friend talk about Kung Fu and flying man Meditation etc. till that age there was nothing like (sannyasi) recluse in me, but it starts from at age of fourteen I have one more friend he gave me book of Yoga, I did not read the book only check its pictures, and I gave this to my school friend with whom I talk about Kung Fu and flying man, about the age of seventeen my school's friend taught me about one Yoga posture, he also told me if I do this so I will become master mind, so I started doing it, that was holidays time and I was alone at home, I did it whole month, I start in the morning and gets up at evening time, it really improved my mind, one day my friend told me that he heard about a (sannyasi) recluse, went to his ashram, bought lots of books, I read (sannyasi) recluse's biography, in his biography he mentioned that he spend month in small box he renounces everything even his family to become sannyasi, I was thinking all the time, he has become sannyasi recluse by austerity, but this seems impossible to me, because I never imagine this kind of life, I was in my teenage, I did not see like yet, how can I renounce everything, it is not about renouncing, from my inside I was not able to accept.

But one day my same friend gave me the Osho's book, when I read this book, I went to deep meditation itself, and end of age of twenty-nine and starting of thirty sannyasin happened with me, this event change everything, before this event, I used to think whatever knowledge I have gathered is my enemy because I was in middle not (sannyasi) recluse and regular, I used to think that someone tells me that fate is true or it is just my misconception, but when I sannyasin happen with me so this fate of was reason of sannyasin, one day I was in meditation and in deep meditation I found the answer my question that fate is great truth, no one can apart from this, this whole existence bonds with fate.